THE OPTIMISTIC TRADITION
AND AMERICAN YOUTH

THE OPTIMISTIC TRADITION

AND AMERICAN YOUTH

Columbia University. Conservation of
Human Resources Project.

BY ELI GINZBERG

with James K. Anderson and John L. Herma

COLUMBIA UNIVERSITY PRESS

NEW YORK AND LONDON 1962

Copyright © 1962 Columbia University Press
Library of Congress Catalog Card Number: 62-19173
Manufactured in the United States of America

To the Memory of

SOL W. GINSBURG

CONSERVATION OF HUMAN RESOURCES PROJECT

The Conservation of Human Resources Project was established by General Dwight D. Eisenhower at Columbia University in 1950 to undertake basic research in human resources. It has been supported by grants from corporations, foundations, and the federal government. The vice-president of the university exercises administrative supervision over the Project.

FOREWORD

In June, 1959, the Field Foundation made a grant to the Conservation of Human Resources Project at Columbia University for the purpose of enabling it to distill selective findings growing out of its more than two decades of basic research on human resources. This grant was precipitated by the 1960 Golden Anniversary White House Conference on Children and Youth. The Foundation hoped in this manner to make the Project's pertinent research findings more readily available to the many professional and lay individuals and groups concerned with the improvement of youth.

As the bibliography at the end of the volume indicates, most of the books incorporating the findings of our research are still in print and we therefore will not repeat, even in summary, what can readily be found in these published materials.

This book, while based on our prior research, has a purpose and structure of its own. We have sought to identify and evaluate the basic stance of our society towards the improvement of youth—particularly how its assumptions about and aspirations for youth are related to what is known about human development and about the institutions that our society has fashioned to further them.

Major General Howard McC. Snyder, advisor to the

Conservation of Human Resources Project, who was instrumental in securing the grant from the Field Foundation, has read the manuscript in its entirety and has enhanced it by valuable suggestions.

While he was unable to participate in the preparation of this book, Dr. Sol W. Ginsburg, to whose memory it is dedicated, played a strategic role in most of the research on which it is based. No one, in our opinion, has made a greater contribution to building bridges between dynamic psychology and the social reality with which this volume is so largely concerned than Dr. Ginsburg, whose premature death took from us a valued colleague, counselor, and friend.

Mr. Alfred S. Eichner contributed greatly to the readability of this volume through his skillful editorial work. I am indebted to the Graduate School of Business of Columbia University for making Mr. Eichner available for this assignment.

ELI GINZBERG
*Director, Conservation of Human
Resources Project*

May, 1962

CONTENTS

THE OPTIMISTIC TRADITION

AND AMERICAN YOUTH

THE NEED FOR PERSPECTIVE

For most of the time that man has been on earth, parents and teachers have had few questions about the raising of children. They have proceeded on the assumption that they should follow the same precepts as those followed by their parents and teachers. True, the outcome might not always be satisfactory. Some youngsters would fail to learn what they were taught and others might exhibit, when they grew up, serious defects. But then, no system of growth and development could be expected to yield perfect results. Some human beings, and some plants and animals as well, will develop serious imperfections, no matter how favorable the circumstances under which they are reared. And the circumstances are frequently unfavorable—insufficient food, space, and other conditions requisite for proper growth and development.

The last century or so has witnessed, at least in Europe and the United States, the increasing mastery by man over the environment which formerly held him prisoner. This, in turn, has given him a growing interest in the improvement of youth, for he has had vastly greater opportunities than did his parents and his grandparents to alter and change—even in a revolutionary way—the conditions under which he rears his children. He is no longer under the necessity of following the practices and procedures of an earlier day.

Vast new possibilities lie open before him. It is small wonder, then, that the past several decades, especially in the United States, have seen a heightened preoccupation with all matters affecting the development and education of the young.

Until recently, the upbringing of the young was no intellectual challenge. One did as one had earlier been done to. In societies where tradition was reinforced by religious sanctions, it was a rare man indeed who questioned the accustomed ways of rearing the young. And if someone hit upon a new approach, it was still rarer for him to put his new insights into practice.

How different the contemporary scene! Hardly a day passes without some authority in one of the learned disciplines, be it medicine, sociology, or education, putting forward a radically new idea about the way in which children should be brought up and educated. Hardly a day passes without some candidate for public office recommending the passage of a law aimed at altering in some important way the basic structure of society and the environment in which children are reared. And hardly a day passes without some critic coming forward with far-reaching proposals to reshape the educational system or some other fundamental institution affecting the young.

It is difficult for us to appreciate, since we take this tolerance towards change so much for granted, how unusual our national stance really is, especially in the area of child-rearing. One would be hard pressed to find, except in brief periods of revolutionary turmoil, any other people so little constricted by orthodoxy about the development and education of the young, other than the orthodoxy that through the advancement of knowledge, improvement in the general environment, and strengthening of educational institutions the job can be done much better than in the past.

It is easier for a society such as ours to commit itself to the improvement of youth than it is for it to gain insight and perspective as how best to gain that objective. For if the improvement of youth depends upon distinguishing between sound and unsound ideas, upon establishing priorities as between competing objectives, and upon making choices within the framework of existing institutions, the task is indeed a difficult one and the need for perspective paramount. The problem is made more difficult by the fact that ideas, social conditions, and specific institutions continue to undergo rapid change in response to forces and influences that have little or nothing to do directly with the improvement of youth. We are fortunate that in a world of increasingly rapid and radical change we are so deeply committed to a positive view toward that phenomenon. While this underlying commitment is a source of strength, it is not, of and by itself, adequate to insure that we will make the most of the opportunities for improvement that present themselves. There is no escaping the need to assess the alternatives that changed circumstances bring into purview; nor is there any automatic method of assessing the relative effectiveness of the various ways we can accomplish our chosen objectives. Committed we may be to the improvement of youth. Enthusiastic we may be about the novel and the new. But commitment and enthusiasm are by themselves inadequate for the task at hand—a task that we cannot escape if we would. There are no easy or self-evident answers to the question of how youth can be improved. We need help in finding our way through the great welter of competing ideas, in properly assessing the probable gains and losses from seeking to alter the environment in which young people are brought up, in understanding the limitations to bringing about constructive changes in those institutions which play so pervasive a role in the development of the young.

Among the unique phenomena of American democracy is the fact that education is everybody's business, though clearly not all people, not even the majority, are likely to be sufficiently knowledgeable that they can formulate independent judgments about the best methods for accomplishing specific educational objectives. But this attitude does throw light on the historic role of the public in shaping our educational system. The public has long considered it its right and duty to determine the amount and type of educational opportunities that are made available, and the public has deemed it its right and duty to determine the conditions under which these opportunities are offered.

Within the domain of public action lie such basic matters as appropriations for buildings, staff, and supplies; the election or appointment of a superintendent; the establishment of policies and procedures for the hiring, promotion, and discharge of teachers; even the approval of broad curricula. But there comes a point—and it is reached rather early—when neither the body politic through the ballot box nor its elected representatives through law can constructively intervene in the educational process. Responsibility for instruction must, of necessity, be centered in the professional educational staff.

And so there has long been, and there will long continue to be, an unstable equilibrium between the public's role and the specialist's in determining the manner in which the educational system makes its contribution to the development of the young. This is one of the most persistently complex problems facing the American democracy, with its dedication to the improvement of youth.

With the broadening of the educational structure, the armed forces and industry have become increasingly prominent in the instruction of both youth and adults. Hence the question of who determines what is taught assumes an even greater urgency. A democracy cannot long survive if the public or any large segment thereof is subjected to indoctrination without its own consent. The fact that business is concerned with the making of money and the armed services with defense does not justify either submitting its captive audience to ideological and political indoctrination under the guise of education.

It is often easier to recognize the economic and social conditions that affect the development of youth than it is to determine how best to utilize additional funds in their behalf. Increasing the expenditures for one program or another, no matter how worthwhile, always involves costs. Were it not for this fact, there are many programs that would long since have been placed on the statute books.

However, the commitment of our society to the improvement of youth does not stand alone. Our society has a wide range of commitments, such as improving the opportunities for the handicapped and the aged. The body politic and its elected representatives are constantly confronted with the need to assess the net social gain from additional efforts in one direction as opposed to another. It simply is not possible, even for a society as rich as ours, to pursue simultaneously and at an optimum speed the realization of every socially desirable objective. Hence, the public needs to know the potential costs and benefits from various programs so that it can better allocate its resources. And since the

potentialities for constructive action are constantly changing in response to changes in knowledge, social conditions,
and the institutions dealing with youth, the public's need
for perspective and guidance can never be satisfied but represents an ongoing challenge to the students of human behavior.

The avidity for the new that has characterized so many
aspects of American life and the enthusiasm so many sectors
have demonstrated in putting a new idea into action have
tended to obscure the sizable gap that exists between ideas,
policies, and implementation. Only a very pragmatic and
experimentally inclined people would assume, as Americans
are likely to do, that every attractive new idea ought immediately to be translated into policy, and that in turn
every new policy should immediately be translated into action, even if it requires major changes in existing institutions.

The processes of human growth and development are so
complex that it requires a high order of faith to assume that
every new idea should be incorporated into policy. Admittedly only those ideas which have been tested, or which
have succeeded in gaining widespread approval, are under
consideration. But the testing of ideas is frequently very
difficult and in most instances considerable time is required
before their validity and usefulness can be reasonably judged.
Moreover, in matters affecting individuals and groups, initial
inquiry does not always result in a clear-cut answer. The
idea under scrutiny may be neither true nor false but may
fall somewhere in between. And falling there, the better
part of wisdom might be to deliberate further on whether
the time is opportune to act on it.

There are additional difficulties that Americans frequently
push aside. Social policy is seldom based on a singular idea.

Customarily it reflects a balance among many ideas, some complementary and some conflicting. This being so, it usually requires considerable thought and effort to determine whether, and in what regard, a policy should be altered to take account of a new idea, assuming that there is widespread agreement as to its validity and potential.

There remains yet another hurdle. Even if the new idea has been incorporated into a new policy, serious difficulties may remain before the new policy can be successfully implemented. Major institutions such as the schools have a history and life of their own and they do not change readily. Professor Paul Mort of Teachers College once remarked that it took about forty years for a proven new idea to be fully accepted by the schools.

The fact that Americans frequently gloss over the difficulties in the translation of a new idea into action is a reflection of their receptiveness to the new and their desire not to put obstacles in its way. In turn, this minimization of the difficulties inherent in implementation provides a more sympathetic environment for the reception of new ideas. A willingness to accept changes frequently exceeds our capacity to bring them about. It is much easier to develop new ideas about how youth should be reared than it is to integrate the new ideas into existing policy. Even assuming that this translation into policy can be made, major troubles remain in getting parents and teachers to change their behavior so that the new policy can be put into practice. To the extent that these observations about the stance of American culture toward new ideas, their incorporation into policy, and their implementation are valid, their pertinency to the theme of the improvement of youth is self-evident.

On each of these fronts there is a need for perspective—

in testing new ideas, in estimating the flexibility of policy, in assessing the practicality of implementation. The improvement of youth can be furthered by faith and courage; without them not much progress can be expected. But faith and courage aided by perspective should prove the more potent, if only because perspective can help so much in pointing out the most promising and productive changes.

* *II*

THE COMMITMENT TO PROGRESS

In his classic study, *Democracy in America*, Alexis de Tocqueville has a chapter entitled, "The Principle of Equality Suggests to the American the Idea of the Indefinite Perfectability of Man." Therein the noted French visitor to American shores says, "It can hardly be believed how many facts naturally flow from the philosophical theory of the indefinite perfectability of man or how strong an influence it exercises even on men who living entirely for the purposes of action and not of thought seem to conform their actions to it, without knowing anything about it."

This chapter will seek to relate the central theme of this book, the improvement of youth, to the fundamental commitment of the American people to the doctrine of perfectability and to lay bare some of the basic values that have given shape and direction to this nation's efforts to encourage the "indefinite faculty of improvement." Unless one recognizes the intensity of this philosophical commitment, it is difficult to appreciate the objectives Americans have set for themselves, the resources they have been willing to invest in the struggle, and the resiliency they have shown when their hopes and aspirations have been temporarily frustrated.

It is not surprising that de Tocqueville saw clearly how deeply the United States, even as early as 1840, was committed to the doctrine of man's perfectability, for the doctrine was, after all, a product of de Tocqueville's homeland. The intellectuals who prepared the way for the French Revolution had attributed the evils from which mankind suffered to bad laws and bad institutions. Change these, they said, and man himself will change. There is no limit to man's potential progress if he has the good fortune to live in a proper environment.

And so it is not surprising to find that deeply imbedded in the American tradition is a firm belief in the power of the environment to mold people for good or bad. This belief in the overriding importance of environment was the almost inevitable consequence of our historical experience. The initial settlers on these shores, as well as the many who came later, gave personal testimony to the influence of environment. They were willing to sunder all ties and run risks on the high seas and in the wilderness in the belief that in the New World they would be able to fashion a better life for themselves and their children. Their belief in the perfectability of man was not garnered from philosophical texts but was a reflection of their personal experience.

Not only were people willing to cross the sea in search of a better environment, but in succeeding generations, right down to our own, millions of Americans have been willing to pull up stakes and move to new regions in the hope that the changed environment will be more conducive to a better life. The New Englanders who settled the Middle West, the Middle Westerners who pushed over the Rockies, the Virginians who moved to the Southwest, all bespeak the deep and abounding faith that Americans have always held in the ability of a more favorable environment to yield them greater satisfactions. The mobility of the

American people did not end with the elimination of the frontier. If anything, it has been intensified during the present century.

The deep faith of Americans in the potency of a favorable environment was closely aligned with a parallel belief in the virtues of hard work. The American environment was not initially favorable—in fact it presented formidable hurdles to those who sought to master it. The Pilgrims almost perished during their first winter, thousands of later immigrants succumbed to the elements, and several hundred years later, in the middle of the nineteenth century, entire wagon trains were decimated while seeking to cross the Rockies.

What happened to people in the forests, on the plains, or in the mountains depended on their ability and willingness to work. Small wonder therefore that work was early placed on a high pedestal in the hierarchy of American values—the very antithesis of Europe, where work, particularly hard manual labor, was considered the curse of the poor man. In their early codes the Pilgrims even limited the amount of time that young children were permitted to play, for play was viewed as the design of the devil to tempt man away from his duty which remained, first and last, hard work—in his own behalf and in behalf of the greater glory of God.

While the changing conditions of American life have somewhat softened this tradition, as well as many of the conditions which nourished it, all ties to the past have not been severed. Secretary Ribicoff only recently talked with deep feeling about the advantage of young boys having a newspaper route so as to learn early in life the value of planning, self-discipline, and hard work.

A marked tension has been developing during the past several decades between the traditional American attitudes toward work and the altered role of work in contemporary society. Among the more difficult and complex aspects of the problem is the search for an appropriate resolution, or at least a tolerable compromise, in respect to the upbringing of children. For the belief that children should learn the virtues of hard work continues to be widely held even though the economy gives increasing evidence of being able to function very effectively without their labors.

During most of our history we subscribed wholeheartedly to a few simple theories about work: A man without a job was not a real man. All honest work was worthy of respect; it mattered little whether a man earned his livelihood by making steel or collecting scrap. The key to a man's worth was the money that he earned with his labor. The strength of these attitudes is reflected in the fact that even today young people from middle-class homes who are attending college may work during the summer vacation waiting on tables, driving trucks, or wielding picks and shovels on a highway construction gang. The tradition runs deep that young people must make their own way; they are not supposed to rely on their parents to provide them with suitable jobs.

There is no need to deny that children born into more affluent homes are better off in the race for advancement than those who first see the light of day in rural shanties or urban slums. Nor need one deny that nepotism has long been part of American life. But the important fact is that the public school was established and expanded to insure that all young people, irrespective of their parents' circumstances, would have a reasonably fair start in life. Large-scale public expenditure for education was the basic test of how sincere Americans were in proclaiming equality of opportunity. While it would not be difficult to demonstrate how far short we fall of meeting this ideal, particularly in rural areas of the South and even more particularly in the case of the Negro, the more striking fact is how well we have succeeded in this unique undertaking. For not only do all children have access to elementary and high schools without cost but in many states they also have access to higher education at little or no expense. While parents may have to forego their offspring's earnings and perhaps even cover part of their living expenses away from home, these are seldom insurmountable barriers.

But opportunity has not been limited only to those who have moved up the educational ladder. With land available to those willing to work it, with industry absorbing all who were able and willing to do a hard day's work, with farmers desirous of the goods that the peddler carried on his back or the storekeeper had on his shelves, the American economy provided strong reinforcement for the tradition that a man, through his own efforts, could determine his own future. The widespread belief in progress was nourished by the reality of progress.

Those refinements of mind and manners that reflected a sheltered and pampered childhood were long scorned by most Americans, not only because they felt ill at ease with the manifestations of European culture, but also because they downgraded the man who had had a favorable start in life. It was like playing with marked cards. For many years, a man running for the presidency who could claim that he had been born in a log cabin had an important advantage.

In a society that expected a man to make his own way, aided only by opportunity as available to all, the corollary doctrine early developed that a man should be free to choose his vocation and his wife, to be master of his own life. While parents had both the right and the responsibility to instill basic values into their children, to help guide them through the difficulties of childhood, they had neither the obligation nor the power to inflict their preferences on their children. Among the liberating forces in the American environment was the abundance of opportunities for all who were willing and able to work. This meant that when a son—though not so clearly a daughter—ran into conflict with his parents, he was generally free to settle the argument by picking himself up and leaving. Once on his own, he became the unquestioned master of his destiny.

Many who came to this country in the nineteenth century had come seeking to escape military service in their homelands. They did not want to spend years under brutal officers, engaged as much in oppressing their fellow citizens struggling for freedom as repelling threatening invaders. The negative attitudes of these more recent immigrants—especially those who flocked to the United States after the abortive revolutions of 1848—found fertile soil for their antimilitary convictions. The old colonists and their descendants also viewed any effort of the federal government to demand service from them in peacetime as a fundamental threat to their freedom. There was deep-seated hostility to the draft during the Civil War, even after the evidence became overwhelming that the North might lose, or that its victory would be indefinitely delayed, unless large numbers were mustered into service. Even at the beginning of World

War I the antidraft tradition was strong enough to lead the government to rely on volunteering, at least at first.

Despite the fact that the United States has had to rely on compulsion to raise manpower for the armed services ever since the mobilization of 1940—except for one short period towards the end of the 1940s—the antimilitary tradition still runs deep in the national consciousness. Many young men still view the prospect of being drafted into military service unfavorably as an unwarranted and surely undesirable interference with their right to choose a career and to prepare for it according to their own preferences.

Choosing a vocation is one of the two major choices in every man's life. The other is his choice of a wife. Here, too, the American tradition speaks out clear and loud. The choice of a spouse is a matter for the individual, and is not to be determined by family or community. Parents may feel strongly on the subject. They may consider the intended spouse unsuitable for their son on any one of a variety of grounds—religious background, ethnic origin, educational achievement, pulchritude, or character—but often there is little they can do to enforce their objections. For the young man can always turn his back on them, find a job, and marry and support the girl of his choice. And while young women may have felt more constrained to heed parental objections, since in earlier decades it was more difficult for them to support themselves and their children if the marriage proved unsuccessful, they too, if they knew their minds and had confidence in their judgment, could follow the dictates of their hearts and ignore their parents. Hence the same environmental factors that helped establish a climate of optimism, material progress, and individualism also made romantic love the foundation for marriage: a young man and woman were to follow their emotions in choosing their life's partner.

Despite the broad sweep of the Declaration of Independence, with its clarion call of life, liberty, and the pursuit of happiness, we now know from a more careful study of our history that there were many groups who, at the establishment of the Republic were not included in its promise. Three quarters of a century had to pass, and a bloody war had to be fought, before slavery was abolished and Negroes had an opportunity to enjoy even minimal rights. And it required more than a century and a quarter after the adoption of the Constitution before women gained full rights of citizenship. Other groups, too, have not always shared fully in this country's liberties or benefits. Despite these serious shortcomings, however, the fact remains that American democracy has been able to afford increasing opportunities to all youth, including those of minority groups.

Around the turn of this century or shortly thereafter, it became increasingly clear that if this nation's commitment to progress was to be more than empty rhetoric the populace would have to be made aware of the constantly expanding opportunities that were opening up, so as to best take advantage of them. For the average citizen, it was hard to keep pace with all that was happening. So much was new and so much was beyond the reach of his knowledge and experience. The ex-farmer found the city a confining place; the immigrant was overwhelmed by much that he encountered in the new land; parents found it difficult to advise their youngsters about occupations unknown to them. Many new jobs were being created in the forward rush of industrialization, but youngsters had no easy way of knowing how to qualify themselves for these jobs and their parents were likely to be no better informed.

Responding to a very real need, new vocations, advice giving and counseling, began to grow. Intermediaries sought to interpret for the lay public new developments in science, the economy, and the arts. Much of the interpretation had a practical focus: to help parents understand how they could bring up their children more effectively; to help young people better prepare themselves for work and life; to assist newcomers to the city to overcome particular handicaps in their background. In more recent years the gap between the expert and the layman has grown even wider, reflecting in particular the accelerated rate at which new knowledge is accumulating and the parallel specialization that has accompanied this development. Correspondingly, the need for guidance has increased and the demand for interpreters has multiplied.

The commitment to progress runs deep in the American story. Not all groups have subscribed to it, but the vast majority have given it their unquestioned allegiance. In fact it has been embraced so enthusiastically that the exaggerations and excrescences—the usual concomitants of enthusiasm—have not always been noted or corrected. The most important of these should at least be briefly indicated.

The doctrine of perfectability, without modification or limitation, is itself subject to serious criticism. It is one thing to be sufficiently optimistic about the prospects for man to improve through his own efforts his life and works. But it is something else again to hold to the belief that there are no limits to what man can accomplish by way of increasing what is good and beautiful and eliminating that which is bad and ugly. There is no basis for such an unrestricted and unlimited optimism in either history or science. The optimists may still be proven correct, but the weight of evidence is against them.

Basic to the belief in perfectability is a rampant environmentalism. This, in its unrestricted form, is a belief that everything bad can be eradicated by improving the environment. Here, too, the extreme position is untenable. Men are born defective and their defects are carried in their genes. Neither sterilization nor death of all defective adults —as Hitler in his wilder plans contemplated—is the answer. For everybody carries defective genes within him which, if joined with those of others, may produce infants with overt defects. And, as every reader of the daily newspaper knows, the chance of unfavorable mutation has vastly increased of late.

There is further ground for uneasiness about an unlimited commitment to progress. The very institutions that a society constructs to accomplish particular objectives, even those primarily focused on the effective development of the young, cannot hope to do more than benefit the vast majority. This may still leave a minority neglected and unaided.

Finally, in the presence of only imperfect knowledge about human beings and about social institutions, no society, no matter how committed to progress, will be able to reshape the environment in a manner that will insure the elimination of all that is unsatisfactory. At best, it can only work at the margins, shifting from the less to the more desirable paths as its knowledge about and control over the environment increases.

The nation's progress has been substantially abetted by the faith of most Americans in the doctrine of perfectability. It was this faith that encouraged and sustained them to put forth the great effort and energy required to reshape the environment so as to make this a better country in which to work and live. Although environmental change has limited rather than unlimited potential for good, the constructive role of the perfectability doctrine in our national experience must be recognized. But its constructive influence must not be permitted to hide its inherent limitations.

* III

OPENNESS TO CHANGE

The commitment to progress based on the belief in man's perfectability, which was so characteristic of American society, carried with it the implication of a positive attitude towards change. In fact, only a society that welcomed innovation, that preferred the new over the old, could bring about fundamental changes in the environment which were necessary for the realization of progress.

These attitudes, to us, appear only natural but in fact they are quite unusual. Almost every society that man had earlier developed had powerful institutions, folkways, and traditions whose primary, if not sole, purpose was to maintain continuity in thought and action—in short, to preserve the ways of the past. Every previous society was basically oriented towards the past, with any pressure to change seen as a serious threat to harmony and survival. How different is the American scene, where the orientation is primarily toward the future, where most customs and institutions have been looked upon as being imperfect and therefore in need of change.

It is misleading, however, to think that a society can be exclusively future oriented, for the younger generation must be formed, to some extent, in the image of the older. To accomplish this, a society must of necessity rely upon deeply entrenched institutions such as home, school, church, armed forces, community organizations—all of which are inherently conservative. It would be a misreading of American history, therefore, to argue that the entire society was at all times future oriented. The truth is that during the long years that the nation was taking shape—that is until the frontier came to an end towards the close of the nineteenth century—there was a safety valve for those who found the old ways too restrictive. They could always break out of their conventional surroundings and seek their fortunes in distant parts where they would not be shackled to the past. And this is what often happened. The young, the restless, the discontented, the adventurers, the gamblers, and many more who felt oppressed by tradition took off in successive generations for places beyond the frontier, while the more stolid and stable remained behind. But those with an eye to the future, who were expanding the frontiers of the new nation, needed the help and encouragement of those who remained behind and the ties between them were never severed. Hence, even the more conservative Easterner was affected in a great many ways by the dynamism of the frontiersman.

Political as well as geographic factors contributed to the general tolerance toward change. The Constitution itself had reserved for the individual states and for the people acting through voluntary organizations certain broad powers. As Justice Holmes and Justice Brandeis later emphasized in a long line of Supreme Court opinions, a major strength of this nation was the power given the individual states for social and political experimentation. All that one need do to appreciate the different legacies of the American and French Revolutions is to contrast the extreme centralization of French education with the diverse conditions prevailing in our fifty states. At any time in the day, every student in the same grade in a French school is pursuing the same lessson, from the same book, with the teacher using the same guide.

Many years ago Goethe wrote in Faust:

> America you have it better.
> No sarcophagi and no castles.

When one considers a people without tombs and castles who deliberately cut themselves off from the past, who had faith in their capacity to build a better world, who were favored by Providence with a land of great potential riches, and who early discovered that they could through hard labor shape a better future for themselves and their children, it is no longer surprising that Americans developed a negative view of the old and a positive view of the new.

It was inevitable that the general tolerance toward change would be reflected in attitudes toward young people. For a society cannot escape the necessity of choosing whether, and to what extent, it will strive to model the next generation in its own image. Once committed to making the future different from the past, a nation must then consider in what regard it is willing to facilitate the next generation's growing up and developing differently. Possessing as it does both the responsibility and the authority for guiding young people through maturity, a society dedicated to change must be willing to assume a critical attitude toward many of its own basic experiences and must further be willing to restrict its own authority in favor of newer, radical ideas. In fact the test of a society's dedication to change is its willingness to experiment in the rearing of its young. Only to the extent that young people are brought up differently from their parents can a society seriously hope to fashion a world that is better.

The extent to which this commitment to progress has resulted in a tolerance toward change in the rearing and education of the young is shown in many ways. A book that has had considerable impact in orienting new mothers to the physiological needs of newborns is entitled *The Rights of Infants*, a title quite unusual in a culture where rights and adulthood are synonomous. The same attitude is reflected in an exchange which occurred recently between the leader of a group of ten-year-olds and an attendant who told them that they could not play in the playground on Sundays. When the youngsters argued that they were busy in school all week and hence that Sunday was the best day for them to play, the attendant, beating a retreat, remarked that he didn't make the rules. The leader of the group then responded, "Then, I'll write to my congressman!" That infants and children have rights in the United States is widely accepted. It is rare, for example, for an American adult to interfere when boys fight. No European, on the other hand, could maintain his self-respect if he did not interfere and put an end to a fight among juveniles.

While it would be foolish to deny that mishandling of children by parents and others exists in our society, the barriers against serious abuse are substantial and are constantly increasing. For instance, it is rare to see a relative pinch a child's cheek as a sign of recognition or affection—a most frequent occurrence in many European societies where it is not necessary to consider to the same degree the rights of the child.

It is interesting to speculate about the circumstances that have contributed to this increasing attention to and respect for the needs, desires, and rights of children. Much of the explanation must lie in the distinctive way in which this country developed. Mobility of population, as previously mentioned, undoubtedly left its mark. In addition, there developed in the United States the nuclear rather than the extended family. This meant that the child did not have to meet the expressed and latent expectations of a long line of relatives—grandparents, uncles and aunts, cousins, and others more distantly removed. In turn, the children's parents had more scope for independent action. If they decided upon one or another innovation in the rearing of their young, they did not have to face criticism from their peers and elders.

Mobility had a further consequence. A parent's previous stock of knowledge and experience was not always relevant in the new environment in which he often found himself. Frequently he had to acquire new ideas which, if they had not completely proven themselves, were at least in favor among those already settled. This reflected itself not only in the behavior of parents, but also in the behavior of their offspring. Tension between the generations is the way of the world but usually the young are made to conform because they are forced to acknowledge, since they have no alternative, the authority of their elders. But in the American environment many parents, by what they did as well as what they failed to do, indicated to their youngsters their own uncertainty. This, in turn, helped further to undermine their authority.

In America parents not only lacked the weight of family tradition but also the weight of those institutions which in more traditional cultures do so much to uphold the authority of the *status quo*, including the authority of parents.

In some communities the church did proffer support, but with so many churches in competition with each other, no single church could wield unquestioned authority. Moreover, school and church were seldom under the same auspices. This meant that the weight of authority outside the family was more diffuse and therefore less potent.

The absence of a rigid class or caste system was also important in loosening the bonds of traditional authority. Parents could not point to the squire or the industrialist and bring their obstreperous children to heel by telling them to do as "their betters" expected them to do. For in America, no man was by birth, or even by accomplishment, the better of any other man. Only the willingness of free men to place political or administrative responsibility in the hands of elected or appointed officials established a hierarchy of power. It was a very unstable arrangement, since what free men granted they could also take away.

While civilizations that live close to the margin of subsistence have on occasion developed warm and supportive attitudes towards children, especially very young children, in general poverty is not a favorable backdrop for humane relationships between men. Except during the earliest years of settlement, Americans have not been hard-pressed to feed their families. Food was generally easy to raise, and with lumber in abundant supply, housing offered no overwhelming problem. These margins of economic freedom undoubtedly enabled American parents to look upon the young as a blessing, rather than a liability. And there were economic as well as sentimental reasons for such an attitude. For as children approached their teens, and frequently even before, they contributed in labor more than they consumed.

Thus, for a great many reasons, reflecting the unique historical, geographical, and economic development of the country, the rigid relationship between parent and child so typical of European society, predicated as it was on the unquestioned authority of the parent, was not duplicated in the New World.

A serious dent having been made in the untrammeled exercise of parental authority, the question naturally arises as to the consequences that ensued. These can be traced to the realm of ideas, experimentation, and counseling—in fact to all the major facets of child-rearing.

In a homogeneous culture with well-established institutions, the younger members of the community in the process of growing up absorb what is considered right and proper as well as learn what is disapproved and censurable. But the situation is less clear-cut in the type of society which, for a long time, has characterized the United States, where different ethnic and religious groups live side by side, where old settlers are intermingled with new immigrants, where class lines are so blurred that they can hardly be distinguished. In such a setting, it is difficult for the members of any group to hold firm to their own particular values. Every day some of these are likely to be challenged by neighbors with different values.

These challenges take place not only in the realm of values but also in the realm of behavior. The ways of neighbors and strangers may appear to be better than one's own, at least as far as one can superficially tell. And so there arises, in the highly pluralistic culture that is ours, with its absence of a ruling class, an established church, or for that matter any other dominant national institution except perhaps the public school, a philosophy of relativism in most matters, including child-rearing. This relativism, however, is skewed in favor of the proposition that there may be much better ways of doing things—more particularly better ways of bringing up one's children than by following the precepts that one learned in Europe or that one gleaned from one's parents who were born in Europe.

To compound matters, one's youngsters are in school for almost as many hours in the day as they are awake at home. During these hours they are subject to indoctrination, direct and indirect, from teachers and peers. It is inevitable that much of what they are taught and more of what they pick up informally is in contrast, if not in conflict, with what they learn at home. Since young children cannot but be impressed with the authority of their teachers, they are more likely to give the greater credence to what their teachers tell them. And their parents, often as much in awe of the teachers as their children, are as likely as not, when faced with outright competition between their beliefs and those of their children's teachers, to give way, or at least to weaken, in their own convictions. All this adds up to one simple point. Parents are open to new ideas on all matters of child-rearing, the more so if the proponents of the new doctrines are their children's teachers, who by special training and specific function are supposed to be experts in those matters.

The same social forces that helped establish a hospitable environment for new ideas also provided a favorable backdrop for experimentation. One of the great strengths of a pluralistic society is the scope that it provides for groups intent upon trying out new ideas. In such a society, it is not necessary to secure a universal consensus ahead of time nor to wait upon the concurrence of those in power.

When American ingenuity paid off handsomely in industry and business, it gave a great spur to experimentation in the fields of child-rearing and education. Here, too, much hope was pinned on the new, such as a feeding formula, a nursery school, a radical change in curriculum. This predilection for experimentation was, in fact, inevitable, given the prevailing critical attitude toward and distrust of conventional ideas.

Closely aligned to the search for the new is the trend towards increasing reliance on specialists. As long as adults were able to guide their lives and the lives of their children with a few maxims transmitted from the past, they had little need to seek out the opinions and advice of others, even those who devoted their lives to one or another aspect of child development. But once parents became less sure of themselves, once they could no longer trust what they had learned through their own experience, they had to seek help from those likely to be better informed and more competent because they were directly involved in exploring new ideas and new approaches.

The greater reliance that American parents placed on the teacher as their children's guide and counselor was one manifestation of a more general trend. But parents also began seeking expert advice about medicine, diet, psychology, preschool experiences, formal education, leisure time activities, occupational information, and much more. The fact that so many parents were in search of information, interpretation, and reassurance helped to create a substantial demand for the services of experts whose primary role was to communicate effectively with lay people and to give them what they so avidly sought—guideposts to the new that could contribute to the improvement of youth.

The growth of the advice-giving professions was speeded by the development in the United States of mass communication industries: first, the daily and weekly papers; later, the monthly magazines, which came increasingly to center on the problems of the child-rearing wife and mother; finally, radio and television. Rising levels of income and education, moreover, put an increasing number of Americans in the position where they could call upon the services of these experts. This explains why the pamphlets on infant and child care published by the government have sold more copies than any other book, the Bible alone excepted.

While the rise of the expert has helped greatly to guide the layman through the labyrinth of the new, the untried, and the promising, it has by no means completely solved his problem of how to cope with and make use of the ever-accumulating stock of knowledge. The layman still must make a choice among the competing experts available to him. There is no escape from this responsibility, just as there is no escape from the responsibility of choice in the political arena.

But if the layman cannot escape the responsibility of choosing among experts, he can, nonetheless, look forward to receiving considerable help from them. For they are frequently in a position to distinguish more clearly between the relative advantages of old and new ideas and thus to determine the practicality of putting new ideas into practice. If this nation's commitment to progress is to endure, then even greater reliance will have to be placed upon the expert in the future, to help the layman find his way through the new areas of knowledge. As long as the population is sufficiently well-educated to make some reasonable estimate of the experts' competing claims, and as long as free competition in ideas continues to prevail in the public domain, a public dedicated to progress will find the road ahead difficult, but passable.

But concern and care will have to be exercised to insure that the preconditions for intelligent choice are established and maintained. The United States has never been particularly friendly to individuals whose primary concern is with criticism. We have been restive about individuals whose metier is to point out the strengths and, alas more frequently, the weaknesses of others. Such activity is likely to be viewed as interfering with progress, by suggesting that no action may be the preferred alternative. In short, the public's ability to choose among experts will, in the first instance, depend on the growth and flowering of a critical tradition.

Secondly, it will depend on insuring that the media of mass communications do in fact, not only in theory, remain open. The merger movement among newspapers, the increasing reliance on syndicated columns, the inability of many established magazines to keep afloat, the unsolved problems of the mass distribution of paperback books, the costliness of time on television and radio, all point to the very real problems of keeping the communication channels open. But the problem becomes vastly more complex once the powerful engines of advertising and publicity begin to operate, to establish and maintain the reputation of certain experts. The ability of Americans to choose intelligently among competing experts will, in the last analysis, depend on the extent to which their education provides them with a critical sense.

* IV

THE NEW PSYCHOLOGY

Of all the intellectual developments in the twentieth century none has had a more direct and widespread influence on the theories and practices of child-rearing than what can be subsumed under the heading of the new psychology. Because the term "the new psychology" does not have accepted usage, let us first say very briefly what it covers. It includes a series of approaches to the study of thought, emotions, and behavior that stand in sharp contrast to theories of an earlier day when psychology was just beginning to emancipate itself from philosophy, on the one hand, and a preoccupation with vision, the study of traits, and the functioning of sense organs, on the other.

Encompassed under the term "the new psychology" are the important contributions starting around the turn of this century of developmental psychology, psychiatry, and psychoanalysis to the widened understanding of emotional growth and development, learning, and intellectual functioning. These major areas can be distinguished from each other, from such related fields as intelligence testing and child psychiatry, and from specific schools of psychoanalytic thought. But for the purpose at hand, which is to trace the impact of the new psychological ideas on social thought and behavior, it is preferable to deal with the several currents as a single stream.

The first question that suggests itself is how did it happen that the American environment in particular proved so receptive to the new ideas, or at least to many of them?

A partial answer lies in the weakening of the traditional belief in revealed religion, which left the moral underpinnings of Western society greatly in need of shoring up. For more than fifteen hundred years, Europeans had found in religious teaching their basic guideposts to conduct. However much individuals had deviated from the teachings of the church, neither the leaders nor the masses had any serious questions about the basic principles of human conduct.

However, in the second half of the nineteenth century, a major assault on the truth of revelation destroyed this foundation of ethical conduct. And many who had lost their traditional faith were in search of a new one. At a minimum they wanted something to replace what the critical approach to biblical scholarship and the evolutionary doctrines of Darwin had shaken.

The fact that the new psychology was a "scientific" discipline based on rationality and buttressed by experimentation helped greatly to heighten its prestige and to facilitate its acceptance. For the decline in religious belief was paralleled by a deepened respect for science. Many developments in psychology required the use of laboratory techniques and procedures so that it was not long before the prestige of the natural sciences began to rub off on the new discipline.

While this ideological shift was probably the main factor in the receptiveness to the new psychology, other factors also played an important role, particularly in the United States where rapid changes in the social fabric left many unresolved tensions between past and present.

As has been pointed out earlier, the United States was to

a marked degree a child-centered culture even before the rise of the new psychology, and as such it had long been restive toward orthodox Calvinist doctrine with its emphasis on predestination and evil. Many Americans did not find it congenial to look upon the behavior of children as something inherently evil. The new psychology with its emphasis on the "naturalness" of child behavior provided a welcome alternative to dour theological doctrines stressing the intrinsic evil in child and man.

Freudian psychology with its focus on the role of sexuality in human life also became part of the struggle, then under way, to win full rights—both social and political—for women. For Freud's contention that lack of normal sexuality would lead to egregious difficulties in human adjustment provided intellectual ammunition for those seeking acceptance of woman as a whole person with a wide range of feelings, desires, and needs of her own.

Finally, as an increasingly productive economic system provided the public with more and more resources to invest in schooling, the question of whether these resources were being used most advantageously arose. With the passage of every year, it became increasingly clear that conventional theories of learning were a weak base on which to erect a much enlarged and hopefully also a much improved educational structure. The strict authoritarian approach, with the teacher putting new knowledge before the child and drilling it into him, frequently with the aid of a hickory stick, began to impress many Americans as a somewhat doubtful and inefficient method. Hence, they were on the lookout for theories of child development and learning which might provide a more satisfactory basis for restructuring the school. And the new psychology seemed to meet this need. For it threw important light on learning at the same time that it established a connection between the development of the child's personality and motivations and on his acquisition of knowledge and skills. Dewey's stress on interests was strongly reinforced by Freud's emphasis on emotions.

The thrust of the new psychology was in four major directions. First, it focused attention on the overriding importance of the family situation in the development of the child's personality. The key to emotional development, the new psychology pointed out, was the individual's experiences during infancy and early childhood—above all else his relationship with his mother, father, and siblings. Emotional disturbance in later life was almost always rooted in a trauma experienced during childhood. Second, the new psychology took a more favorable view toward human potential. In contrast to the early geneticists who had placed major emphasis on heredity, the new psychology said that the processes of development, particularly emotional development, determined whether individuals would be encouraged to make the most of their aptitudes. While the new psychology stopped short of saying that the level of human accomplishment was solely a matter of early conditioning—a position developed by Watson and other behaviorists—it nonetheless held that the quality of the environment was a major determinant of later performance.

Probably the most revolutionary effect of the new psychology was to force a radical shift in the attitude towards child behavior. Since so much of what children did was at variance with adult standards, it had long been dealt with by repressive methods. By stressing the extent to which child behavior was dictated by natural drives, the new psychology shifted the focus from a moralistic to a naturalistic basis. This shift was part of a much broader social movement whereby religious and moralistic interpretations were increasingly superseded by scientific and naturalistic explanations.

Finally, the new psychology provided an understanding of the ways in which emotional disturbance in later life was linked to defects in the developmental process. The inability of a child to concentrate in school, the excessive shyness of an adolescent, the alcoholic proclivities of an adult could, for the first time in the history of human thought, be understood by tracing them to the emotionally disturbing and distressing experiences in the earliest years of a person's life. If the child was deprived of a mother's love, if he was treated as a baby beyond infanthood, if he grew up in terror of a domineering and harsh father, if he was the continued butt of an older sibling's hostility—if he experienced any such trauma, he would likely manifest serious emotional disturbance that would interfere with his ability to function effectively or gain satisfaction from life. Here were important new vistas. But first the new theories had to be adopted and applied.

With the realization that most child behavior was the expression of instinctual drives, parents and educators began to adopt an attitude of permissiveness rather than of restriction and frustration. Instead of trying to prevent children from expressing themselves—which had long been the accepted practice—the experts now argued strongly in favor of avoiding frustration by permitting each child the maximum degree of freedom to express himself. The turnaround was complete: parents hesitated to establish any limits, even when they recognized physical dangers in not doing so, for they stood in fear of stunting the child's sound emotional development.

The new psychology played a major role in freeing American society from its prudish attitudes towards sex, an inheritance from its religious and, more particularly, its Calvinist tradition. The theory that sex was normal and natural, that children had sexual interests and desires, and that nothing could be gained but much might be lost by harsh repression of these instinctual proclivities helped bring about a more tolerant attitude toward relations between the sexes. Coeducational schools had long been accepted, if only for economic reasons. It was simply not practical, outside of large population centers, to provide separate schools for boys and girls. But the new attitudes towards sex went much further. No longer did it appear necessary or even desirable that parents should keep girls and boys apart. Just the reverse was true. Boys and girls were given increasing opportunities to meet and get to know each other. In place of the long-established tradition of denying sex, or at least fearing it because of its connection with the doctrine of original sin, the new psychology produced what can only be called a positive attitude toward the long-forbidden subject.

Since the new psychology traced emotional development through a series of stages, each with a potential for crisis, parents, teachers, and others in authority became much more understanding of aberrant behavior. When a child of three suddenly developed what seemed to be excessive stubbornness, when eight-year olds would have nothing to do with members of the opposite sex except perhaps to torment them, when adolescents became excessively moody so that a parent could not ask a simple question without receiving an uncivil reply—when these and similar types of "bad behavior" were encountered, adults were no longer deeply disturbed. They had come to recognize, from the teachings of the new psychology, that these crises were more or less part of normal emotional development, that the more extreme forms of behavior would recede almost as quickly and as unexpectedly as they had originally emerged.

Understanding led to changes in action. Sanctions formerly applied to unruly children were now withheld. Parents became less insistent on the child's conforming to their own standard of behavior. They recognized that even with the best will in the world, a child going through a difficult stage in his emotional development needed toleration and possibly even special support.

The new psychology had further impact. It led to an increased demand for psychotherapists and others skilled in the diagnosis and treatment of emotional disorders. Many children with emotional difficulties, it was realized, could be helped by these experts, particularly when they were in a period of special tension. As time went on, this type of assistance was even provided by others besides the psychotherapists, for the new psychology became part of the training of other specialists—physicians, teachers, social workers, and ministers. With their broadened and deepened insights, many of these specialists were able to see more clearly and to act more wisely than laymen in dealing with young people experiencing emotional difficulty. In the case of pediatricians and nursery school teachers, the new psychology, in particular, revolutionized their approaches and techniques.

The new insights also led to radical changes in child rearing within the home and in pedagogy within the school. Previously, parents and educators had relied on their authority as adults to impress upon the young the right way of doing things. Whenever this failed, they resorted to punishment, physical and otherwise. That infants and very young children might not yet possess the minimum degree of understanding required to comply with the demands made of them had, of course, been appreciated. But once the age of understanding had been reached, children were likely to be held strictly to account. If they failed to do what they were told, the pain of punishment, it was felt, would sharpen their memories and lead to correct behavior in the future.

The new psychology, however, showed that establishing an environment of love and security was more important and crucial to healthy emotional development, especially for the infant and the young child. It also shed light on the important role that certain adults play in the emotional development of children by serving as their models. Drawing on these new ideas, parents, teachers and others involved in child development came to appreciate that fear of punishment was one of the least desirable methods of controlling behavior. Many young people, for example, could be encouraged to do something difficult or disagreeable if asked to do so by somebody who loved them. For, to retain the love of those whom they love in turn, children can, if put to the test, call on hidden resources to surmount difficult situations. Similarly, young people, in the process of growing up, need to model themselves after adults whom they love. They, too, can be encouraged to do much that they might otherwise avoid because it is difficult, disagreeable, or takes them away from something that is fun, if they come to appreciate that the behavior required of them is an essential step in their efforts to grow up in accordance with the model set up for them.

The new psychology led to the awareness that there were important instinctual energies that could be harnessed to get children to study and to learn. Children had interests of their own, the new psychology pointed out. If given an opportunity to gratify these interests, at least in part, within the school, they could more easily be taught. Clearly, it was better for young people to learn because of interest than out of fear.

Other types of motivation, it was discovered, could also be used to encourage learning, such as the thrill of competition, the desire for group acceptance, and the drive for self-expression. These and many more motivations were slowly harnessed for use in various facets of child-rearing, particularly in education.

One important aspect of the new psychology was to bring the study of man within the orbit of scientific inquiry. This was a radical change from earlier generations. As long as man was viewed as the unique creation of a Divine Being, a powerful barrier stood against treating him as a natural phenomenon subject to systematic study like the stars, rocks, or animals. Once Darwin established the link between other members of the animal kingdom and man, scientists no longer hesitated to apply the tools of science to the study of human behavior. The new psychology appeared on the scene at a particularly propitious moment, when the barriers against the scientific study of man were just in the process of being overcome. This undoubtedly contributed to the advance of the new discipline.

In no field did the theories and techniques of systematic

scientific inquiry have more impact than in the study of intelligence. In France, England, and the United States the first decade of this century saw a rapid advance in the design and standardization of intelligence tests, thanks to men such as Binet, Sanford, Spearman, Thorndike.

These studies of intelligence laid the foundation for a wide range of programs aimed at strengthening the education of youth. They helped to establish the existence in a great many cases of a gap, sometimes large and sometimes small, between the intellectual potential of a child and his actual school performance. On the basis of these and other, more refined analyses of children's intellectual strengths and weaknesses, educational psychologists could help school authorities to place children in learning environments that were more conducive to their intellectual development. Now, for instance, there was a way to determine a child's intellectual potential and assign him to a class where the instruction was geared to his capacity to profit from it. The new testing instruments, moreover, made it possible to spot children whose school achievement was below their tested potential. They could then be given special attention.

The new psychology left a mark upon many crucial aspects of child-rearing and education. The atmosphere in the home was considerably altered. Parents loosened their reins; they became increasingly permissive. The atmosphere in the school was likewise altered. No longer did the teacher rely primarily on his authority as a teacher to force knowledge upon the recalcitrant child. Instead he tried to elicit and hold the interest of the child in the subjects under discussion and in the complete learning process. The atmosphere also changed in the society as a whole. It came to understand more fully the role of instinctual forces, including the sexual ones, in the development of behavior. It also came to understand more fully the nature of emotional disturbances and the steps that could be taken to alleviate or otherwise deal with them.

But not all influences of the new psychology were positive. An infatuation with the new led to extravagances and excesses. Many who had to apply the new knowledge had only a limited understanding of what the scientists and scholars were uncovering. They frequently failed to appreciate all the difficulties of adapting the new knowledge to the problems of every day life, with its complex institutions and multiple objectives. The intervening decades have witnessed an increased acceptance of the new psychology. But the problems that have developed as a result of misunderstanding and misapplication of the new doctrines have not yet been eliminated.

Reducing the extent to which children were dealt with harshly, were forced to conform to adult standards, and were subject to considerable frustration undoubtedly represented a social gain. But some misguided devotees of the new psychology went too far in holding that children should not be frustrated at all. When a young child is given everything he wants, his emotional development is certain to be seriously damaged. Sound growth and development requires that a child do things new and difficult, so that he can build up his capacities and self-confidence. Such learning will inevitably involve many unsuccessful trials. These, in turn, will inevitably lead to frustration. If parents seek to protect him from this frustration, they will deprive him of an important aspect of personality development. For the child who is protected from frustration will grow up not only deficient in skill but also deficient in the emotional resilience he will need to tolerate the inevitable frustrations that are part and parcel of every adult's life, no matter how well-endowed he may be in the gifts of nature or of property.

The frank recognition of the important role played by the instinctual forces, including the sexual ones, also helped to reverse what was often a most unhealthy situation. It helped free the child from fears about feelings that he could not repress. But the liberation that took place often went too far. Men are not animals and the sex drive must be controlled. Many parents, misunderstanding the necessity for limits, failed to set any. They exposed their children to more sexual stimuli than they could successfully cope with; they failed to indicate their disapproval of certain types of sex play; and some even gave young adolescents tacit and overt approval to engage in sexual activity before these youngsters were mature enough to guide their own behavior effectively. In these and in other respects, the new freedom went too far.

The new psychology, furthermore, contributed significantly by alerting parents and teachers to the potential emotional difficulties of certain children. It also helped by pointing out the possibility of successfully treating these children. But the new doctrines also led many adults to believe that it was possible for children to grow up without any significant tensions and problems. Some parents became so enamored with the potentialities of psychotherapy that they were on the phone every day—and in the office almost as frequently—seeking expert advice on how to deal with their children's emotional problems. And there were teachers, social workers, and others in a position to counsel parents who also saw in psychotherapy the only solution for almost any type of problem. Such attitudes were falsely based, on two accounts. First, they frequently saw serious problems where none existed. Some tension and difficulty is inherent in the growing up process. Every child, as he passes through certain stages, must loosen his emotional dependence on those to whom he has been very attached and must learn to cope with new challenges in the world outside his home. While support and reassurance may help if the child begins to experience difficulty, excessive concern can only lead to a heightening of the child's anxieties, making the ultimate resolution of the problem even more difficult. Whether a person successfully copes with his difficulties may often depend on whether he believes that he is supposed to cope with them on his own rather than seek someone else's help.

In broadening our understanding of the maturation process, the new psychology made another important advance. But once again, it was misused. Many parents and teachers feared to use punishment as an instrument, not recognizing that without punishment, effective education is frequently impossible. Why, for example, should a lazy child attend to his homework if he is promoted to the next class regardless of his performance? How can a child engaged in socially disapproved activities recognize that they are disapproved of unless he is punished for his actions? Delinquent behavior must be reprimanded before it can be treated.

Even in the case of intelligence testing, where the applications of the new psychology were relatively less complex, difficulties and errors arose. For one thing, measuring intellectual potential proved much more complex than the early investigators had suspected. Eliminating the effects of a testee's unfavorable environment, it has come to be realized, is not a simple matter. Furthermore, many users of tests, not appreciating the complex nature of intelligence itself, failed to realize that a single measure might not reveal a person's great variety of differing strengths and weaknesses. Then too, some experts for a long time failed to appreciate that intelligence scores, though supposedly reflecting potential, and thus immutable, were actually subject to significant change over time. Finally, judgments based on a test score were not always borne out by later observation. In predicting a person's success in school or at work, counselors frequently gave too little weight to the important role played by interest and motivation.

While these various aspects of the new psychology led to much-needed reforms in child-rearing and education, they were also overgeneralized and sometimes misapplied. As a result, many faulty practices were introduced into the home, the school, and the community at large.

Since the ideas were revolutionary, error was probably inevitable. But today, a half century after they first saw the light of day, confusion is still widespread. In sum, continuing difficulties arise out of three basic failures. The first is the failure to differentiate between understanding behavior and controlling it. The life history of an adolescent may provide good reasons why he committed a crime. But society is still faced with the problem not only of understanding why it was committed but also of what action to take.

The second basic confusion equates education with therapy. Education, by its very nature, involves demands made upon the child, including the acquisition of knowledge, skills, and controls. In the judgment of his elders, these acquisitions are essential to the survival of society. Therapy, on the other hand, to be effective must in large measure be permissive and must elicit the voluntary cooperation of the individual. Unless the child in trouble wants to be helped, nothing can be accomplished. Hence the psychotherapist must often be supportive and noncritical, at least until the individual is somewhat advanced in his treatment.

Finally, widespread misconception results from equating the psychological facets with the whole of life. It is true that emotional considerations are likely to touch every aspect of human life, for humans when they act and react are inevitably subject to psychological forces. But this is not the same as saying that human behavior is determined exclusively by psychological factors. Much of what goes on in the world also reflects the compelling forces of social institutions—how men make a living, when they marry, how many children they have, whether they are called to arms, how their time is divided between work and leisure, when they retire, and even when they die. And what is true of adults is also true of children. Their development, while certainly influenced by psychological forces, is also a reflection of those dominant social forces whose role must never be ignored or minimized.

V

THE TRANSFORMATION OF WORK

In every society the shaping of youth is, in large measure, determined by the responsibilities which these same youth will face in adulthood. Since individual and community survival depends on adults being able to wrest a livelihood from a niggardly nature, work has always stood at the very center of adult life. Its central significance in turn has helped to mold the way in which the young are prepared for the effective discharge of their adult responsibilities.

Children learn about the crucial importance of work at about the same time as they learn the significance of words and numbers. While the child cannot fully appreciate all the ways and values of adults, he can glean certain significant insights surprisingly early. He comes to appreciate, to some degree, that the work that his father does determines the kind of home he lives in, the toys he plays with, the other children he comes in contact with, and much else that influences his daily life. And if his father should by chance lose his job, he will realize even more clearly that work is the key to life.

Even before a child starts school he has become acquainted, without even realizing it, with a great many attitudes about work and its rewards. He has probably sensed from what goes on at home that his father is deeply involved in his work, that he likes his work, views it with distaste, or is somewhat ambivalent toward it, sometimes talking approvingly of it and at other times complaining about it. The young child has also absorbed, however indirectly, how his parents feel about the adequacy of their income, whether they think it is satisfactory or whether they are dissatisfied and look forward to earning more money.

Beyond these considerations, the young child will have had some experience with the performance of household chores, for him a first prototype of adult work. He may be required to tidy up his room, take care of a younger sibling, or help his mother with some task. Today, except among the very poor, children are seldom burdened by heavy duties; but there was a time, not so very long ago, when the demands made on young children for help in the home and on the farm had a permanent influence on their attitudes towards work.

Aside from the home, the child's introduction to the world of work begins in the school. There he receives instruction in that body of essential knowledge without which he cannot effectively meet the demands of adulthood. While the school can employ, as noted in the last chapter, such powerful motivations as interest and the drive for self-expression, it also makes use of adult authority, discipline, standards, and rewards and punishments in order to accomplish its central mission. In fact, it is in school that the child is fundamentally conditioned, as well as prepared, for his later work.

Admittedly the American public school has long viewed its responsibilities as going beyond the task of preparing young people for future work. It has tried to teach young people to accept civic and political duties as well as to participate in cultural and social activities. Basically, however, the school is supposed to give all young people, regardless of their family backgrounds, a reasonably fair start in life to enable them to go as far as their capabilities will take them in the competitive adult race. And this means preparing them for the world of work.

This then is the setting within which children first learn about work. But historical changes have introduced new elements into the situation. In the past, the very pervasiveness of work not only determined how adults and young people spent most of their waking hours, it also helped shape their ideas about life itself. Like the other dominant facets of human experience—family, sex, religion, health, war, and death—work was a basic element in the structuring of society.

An outstanding characteristic of the last half century, especially in the United States and Western Europe, has been the rapid transformation in the nature of work under the impact of modern technology. The result has been a rising discrepancy between traditional attitudes and current behavior with respect to work, a tension reflected not only in the lives of many adults but also in the rearing of the young.

TRADITIONAL STANCE TOWARDS WORK

Deeply ingrained in the American tradition, especially its dominant Puritan strand, is the belief in the essential value of work itself. This belief has religious roots, deriving from the biblical injunction that man shall eat by the sweat of his brow. Hence, work is one way of fulfilling God's commandment.

At the same time there is within our society a deep-rooted suspicion and hostility towards idleness. If work is good, then non-work is bad. And that is a view that long held sway. The Puritans strongly believed that leisure was an invitation for the Devil to tempt man into evil ways, and that the best protection, therefore, was to keep busy doing useful work. Of course, the early colonists' environment reinforced these religious doctrines, for there was little chance of the colonists taming the wilderness unless they were willing to work long and hard.

With work exalted and leisure denigrated, it was only natural that parents should consider it their duty to see to it that their children were early trained for work.

As the school was originally intended to teach young people to read the Scriptures, the early Puritan communities had no difficulty justifying such a diversion from the business of work and salvation. Nor was it difficult for them to justify the later extension of basic education, since it was clear that additional schooling better prepared a man for later work. Moreover, the fact that the school was for the most part an institution where children were held to strict account and punished for their failings helped to assure the dour leaders of the community that education was a serious matter, not a lark or a frolic.

But once a boy had completed his basic schooling, it was felt, he ought to begin working and to keep on working until stopped by physical infirmity or death. The expression, "to die with your boots on," has a particularly American ring. Women were also expected to work and work hard, though their place was in the home and on the farm. It was not considered proper for any but young girls or widows to seek employment out of the home. Still, the fortunes of many a farm and frontier family depended on the general health and skill of the woman of the house.

There were times, of course, when one did less work. But aside from Sundays and important holidays—Fourth of July, Thanksgiving, and Christmas—the rhythm of work was determined mainly by the weather. It eased in winter but there was more than enough even then to keep most men busy.

In striking contrast to the Old World, the New did not make subtle distinctions between the types of work that men performed. In Europe some jobs were held to be appropriate only for gentlemen, others only for the common man. These arbitrary distinctions were deeply ingrained in European countries but in the more fluid American scene they failed to take hold. Here the central question was not necessarily what type of work one did but how successful he was at it. To the extent that distinctions did exist between different types of work they were much less important, for a man of ability could easily rise within his lifetime from a job of little prestige to one of very considerable distinction. The story of Honest Abe, the railsplitter who became President, points up both the frontier attitude toward manual work and the ease with which a talented man could move up the job hierarchy.

One final point: Until shortly before the beginning of the present century, most people lived on the farm where, typically, the family operated as a single economic unit. Whenever the school was not in session, girls and boys worked as much as their age and strength permitted, alongside their parents. This family pattern also prevailed in other sectors of the economy—in handicraft industries carried on in the home, in distribution, and, to a lesser extent, in the many small workshops that played so prominent a part in the economy.

These were the generations that grew up with an intimate and direct knowledge of work. Their years in school were relatively few, and they knew that once they finished school, they were expected to go right to work. But if luck was with them, if they were competent and worked harder than the next man, they or their children could look forward to a better life in the future. In short, work was their fate but it was also the key to advancement. And so work was both a burden and a promise.

MAJOR TRANSFORMATIONS

Since our perspective is limited, it is sometimes difficult to realize the significance of recent changes. This is true of the changes now taking place in the world of work, which cannot fail to have a significant impact of the education and training of youth. While few of these changes have of themselves escaped attention, their cumulative impact may not have been clearly perceived. Nor has the tension between the old ideas and the new reality been fully appreciated.

The first and most startling change is the fact that within the course of the last half century, Americans have come more and more to work for others rather than for themselves. This means they must report to work by a certain time, do what they are told, and remain at work until the end of the shift. During these hours, they must surrender part of that liberty which had come to be the most hallowed possession of free men. Small wonder then that the last few decades have witnessed the working population's continuing efforts to reduce the hours they must work. While there are other explanations for the steady pressure towards shorter hours, such as fear of unemployment and excessive strain, it is doubtful whether these other factors have played so prominent a role as the desire of the average American to increase his freedom to determine his own life.

The change from a substantially rural to a predominately urban society has added momentum to the drive towards shorter hours. The city provides many more opportunities for recreation, especially for families with ever more disposable income at their command, as in fact has been the situation for most Americans throughout most of this century.

The life of married women has, in particular, been eased. Modern technological developments have greatly simplified housekeeping and homemaking. Moreover, substantial reduction in the number of children conceived and born, along with the marked improvements in health and medicine have literally added years to the average life-span of the American female—not to mention the improved quality of those years. No longer is the woman of forty a worn-out drudge, as her grandmother at that age frequently was.

Also, married women now have the option of seeking employment outside the home, part time or full time, after their family responsibilities have lessened. Since the end of World War II, the employment opportunities available to them have been constantly expanding.

Another large group with much to gain from the transformation in the nature of work has been the Negroes. Confined to Southern farms prior to World War I, they were for the most part at the bottom of the employment ladder in this country's most backward and depressed area. A few escaped to the North during and immediately after World War I; however, the Negro made his most substantial gains with the onset of World War II and the two succeeding decades of relatively full employment.

But the recent transformation in the nature of work has also introduced new difficulties for white males, women, and Negroes, just as it has contributed markedly to resolving old ones. Most conspicuously, work has become increasingly professionalized and specialized. This, in turn, has both encouraged and been encouraged by a lengthening of the education and training that young people receive before beginning work. Increasingly, a young person's success in his career is determined by the quantity and quality of his preparation. Access to educational opportunities and the ability to profit from them, therefore, have come to play a major role in determining a man's occupational future. When a man needed only basic literacy plus a little determination to give him a good start in life, it was relatively easy for government to provide the requisite educational opportunities. With attendance at a good college or professional school increasingly important for those who aspire to the higher rungs of the occupational ladder, the question of access to, and the quality of education assumes a much more crucial role in the shaping of a person's occupational future.

Another important dimension of this problem reflects the shift that has taken place from general self-employment to widespread wage and salary employment. The conditions under which men are forced to work for others, that is, the length of time they must work, the wages they are paid, the circumstances under which they are eligible for advancement, and the terms under which they may be discharged—all these take on crucial importance. Because of the individual worker's impotence to affect the decisions of his employer, especially if the employer is a large, impersonal corporation, trade unions and other forms of joint action were developed by the worker to deal with these and other important matters. As a consequence, the individual worker's advancement, be he blue collar, white collar, or junior executive, has come to be highly formalized, with seniority the most important determinant. While the scope for individual initiative has not been completely eliminated, it has been greatly restricted. Consequently, most Americans are now more likely to seek personal gratification off the job than in their work.

Two additional changes should be noted at least briefly. Urban industrial life has, for the most part, brought an end to the family pattern of work. While parents and children still operate as a team in some small retail establishments, most children growing up in a metropolitan area have little to do with the process of earning a livelihood. What is more, in many cases the work which their parents do may be so esoteric—accounting, public relations, or research—that the child has no way of appreciating what is involved. His parents' work remains a mystery. All that he can perceive is how they feel and react to it, to the extent that they reveal this at home through their discussions and their moods.

Finally, recent changes have had the effect of vastly shrinking the place of work in the totality of a man's life —not for all men but for the great majority. No longer does a man work from sunup to sundown, six days a week, with only a few holidays to break the yearly monotony. And no longer does he come home so exhausted that all he can do is stop off at the local bar, then fall into bed after eating his supper. Increasingly, each day is now divided into two—part to be spent on the job, and part off the job. The same division applies to workdays and weekends, to the working part of the year and to the three or four weeks' annual vacation. This radical reduction in the hours of work and in the energy which this work demands has led to a restructuring of adult life which, of necessity, is having a most profound impact on the development of the young.

IMPLICATIONS FOR YOUTH

The first, and perhaps most far reaching consequence of the revolution in work has been the difficulty that young people now have learning about work from their parents. Where their parents work, how they work, the significance of what they do, and much more that used to be part of every farm boy's direct experience now takes place beyond the city child's purview. While the latter still has an opportunity to learn about the work of the storekeeper, the physician, the dentist, the taxi-driver, and many others with whom he comes into contact, the great majority of today's jobs are performed only within buildings to which the urban lad never has access and of which he has no knowledge, much less understanding. While theoretically he can still learn something about work from his father, in practice he is much more apt to learn about leisure-time activities— when they play catch, go to the movies, take a ride in the country, or work in the basement on some models.

The fact that his father brings home with him only a little of his total work experience means that the child gains only a very skewed and unbalanced view of work. Most likely the discussions between his parents will deal with the least pleasant aspects of his father's work, not with its many satisfying elements.

At the same time that work is becoming less and less of a real thing to the young child, his period of preparation for work is being constantly lengthened. Thus, many children find it increasingly difficult to maintain interest in their school work, since they do not see how it affects what they will do after they leave school. At the very time that they are sorely in need of relating their occupational objective to their current school effort, the link between the two is being weakened by most children's remoteness from any actual work experience.

Another facet of this problem is the difficulty many people have in learning about some of the more significant, if esoteric, aspects of the occupational world. It is not easy for a youngster to gain even a preliminary insight into the nature of social science research, computer programming, or metallurgical engineering. These are but a few illustrations of the very complex, demanding types of work that a modern, industrial society requires. None of these careers can even be explored, much less entered, unless the young man has enough interest in education to keep at his studies diligently until he reaches the age of discretion, that is, until he reaches the middle of his college years.

But even those emotionally capable of enduring the long educational preparation required for entrance into many of the more interesting and rewarding fields of work are likely to experience a related difficulty. Preparing for a satisfying occupation runs into conflict with another aspect of the drive towards adulthood and independence—sexual maturity and family formation. In many European countries the conflict was contained, if not solved, by a set of values which allowed young men studying at the university to take care of their sexual needs by informal rather than formal relationships. But this solution has never been favored in the United States. In the area of sexual ethics, the United States has remained bound by tradition.

Currently the tendency in America, especially among those from upper income homes, is towards parental support of young people entering into marriage while one, or both of them, are still in school. Though this does help solve the financial problem, it deepens rather than simplifies the emotional entanglements. For if independence is an index of adulthood, then a marriage subsidized by parents fails to contribute thereto.

The difficulty is further exacerbated for young men by the fact that they must add a third variable to their balancing act. In addition to career and marriage, they must contemplate spending several years in military service. While many young men undoubtedly mature during this period of service, many others profit relatively little from it.

Many, perhaps even most young men are not fully aware of the implications of these conflicting opportunities or pressures—career, marital, and military. But the decisions which they make must inevitably favor one over the other. They cannot all receive the same priority.

The facts that so many young people drop out of high school; that so many fail to enter, or having entered, later drop out of college; that others with considerable potential shy away from professional or graduate training; that many of those eligible for financial assistance to further their education turn their backs on the opportunity—all are symptoms that the transformation in the nature of work has precipitated a host of problems. Among those that we will consider in greater detail are the educational system, the life plans of young people, and the special problems experienced by women and Negroes as they face new career opportunities.

VI

EDUCATION: THE OPEN SESAME

While the public school was initially established to help the children of the Puritan farmers learn to read the Bible, it was not long before the broader values of literacy were recognized. The farmer and craftsman able to read, write, and keep a set of accounts were clearly at an advantage when it came to earning a living.

For many generations this close connection between work and education continued. The school, no matter how much concern it might express for the higher things of life, such as religion, culture, and more recently constructive leisure, never deviated very far from what it always considered its major task, the preparation of young people for their life's work. Any major transformation in the nature of work, therefore, must inevitably lead to major changes in the educational scene. But, in fact, this was just one of many powerful social forces operating in recent decades to alter the structure of the American educational system.

The amount of formal schooling that young people receive has always been related to the economic well-being of their parents. Only the wealthy, in earlier generations, could absorb the cost of keeping young people in school for an extended period of time and at the same time forego the income that they might be earning were they not busy studying. Local governments early in the history of the United

States, by providing free schools close to home, removed the first of these burdens. But no one ever seriously considered public subsidies to parents as a means of eliminating the second. Given this close relationship, then, between family income and educational opportunity, it is not surprising that the recent rise in per capita income levels has coincided with a greater utilization of educational resources.

A second factor, previously alluded to, has been the shift in the nation's economy from agriculture to industry, from the need for unskilled labor to the demand for highly trained personnel. In nineteenth-century America, when new settlements were constantly springing up on the frontier and the ceaseless flow of immigrants was inundating the cities, there was more work than workers—and the labor of young people was an important supplemental resource. But the development of modern industry, such as petrochemicals and electronics, leaves little room for juveniles. These industries require few semiskilled workers and still fewer unskilled workers. This fundamental change in the composition of the labor force has, in turn, reduced the opportunity cost of keeping young people at their studies. If they were not in school, they would be hard pressed to find profitable employment. The Great Depression, when labor sought and secured public support for raising the mandatory school age in the hope of reducing unemployment, further accelerated this tendency.

The campaign to raise the mandatory school age had gained considerable momentum even before the Great Depression. There was, first of all, the insistence of educators that simple literacy was no longer adequate preparation for an increasingly complex world. Secondly, there was the evidence marshaled by reformers that employing children at too early an age stunted their physical and psychological development. Additional factors were the decline in average family size and the rapid growth of the city. The first made it easier for parents to devote more resources to each child and the second made it possible for local governments to provide expanded educational opportunities at lower costs through the resulting economies of scale.

The steadily rising standards for admission to various professional schools have also affected the length of secondary education. Admittedly the two are somewhat interdependent. If the average youngster remains in school for twelve years, a professional school has fewer inhibitions about requiring that he complete another six to eight years before he is qualified to work. But the educational preparation of tomorrow's professional man also depends on what advances are made in the various disciplines and the time required for a young person to master them in depth. Of course, this has its limits, too. For example, it is now realized by some that increasing the years of formal education for a medical career has perhaps exceeded the optimum point, and several leading universities have recently reduced the former nine-year requirement of college, medical school, and internship to a seven-year program.

With more time now available for leisure activities, a new argument has arisen for increasing the conventional years of schooling. Now, it is held, the school must not only help the young person get ahead occupationally but must also enable him to make more constructive use of his leisure time. As a result, the school curriculum has been broadened in recent decades to include instruction in music, drama, painting, and the other arts.

Thus, in our democracy the school has become both the

instrument of its progress and the mirror of its accomplishments. In this country, the school, in response to many
forces, including the rise in living standards, the progress
of science, the transformation of industry, the acceleration
of urbanization, and changes in the role of adult work, has
been undergoing rapid change. But inevitably the school's
response has been uneven. In some areas it has moved radically, in others sluggishly. And in every instance the magni-
tude of the challenges it faced left it with many unsolved
problems.

PROBLEM AREAS

From the increase in the average number of years spent
within its walls come many, if not all, of the difficulties
which the school is now experiencing. There is first the
serious and to date unresolved problem of how the school
can provide a meaningful curriculum for those many adolescents who have never developed an interest in abstract
ideas or who have lost what little interest they once had.
As one solution, the high school has broadened its traditional academic curriculum, now offering something of interest to each group of young people. It has added courses
in various vocational subjects as well as courses in marriage
adjustment, homemaking, child-rearing, and other subjects
that will enable young people to meet the challenges of
adulthood. While this proliferation of the curriculum has
undoubtedly helped to retain the interest of many pupils,
it has fallen far short of its goal.

Educators have found that it is not possible to conduct
a worthwhile industrial-vocational program unless the students have some skill in mathematics and some power of
abstraction. Thus many of those who do not fit into the

academic program also do not fit into the vocational program, and they are shunted instead into one or another
variant of a "general" program. But no school system has
yet fully succeeded in putting together a sufficiently attractive group of courses so that young people of relatively low
intellectual capacity and motivation can be stimulated. If
the pressures from home are substantial, they may remain
in school until they graduate. Otherwise they will drop out
as soon as the state law permits. But even if they do remain
in school, they are apt to get very little out of their time
spent in class.

The blame for this situation is generally placed on the
school. It has failed these youngsters, it is widely felt. This
may be true in some cases but not in most. The simple fact
is, that once a youngster becomes pubescent, adults can
no longer force him to be diligent in his studies. His parents
can prevent him from going to the movies; they can keep
him in his room; they can even make him look at his books.
But they cannot force him to learn. And what is true of
parents is even more true of teachers. It may well be that
educators have not paid sufficient attention to the problem
of the drop-out. But there are strong reasons, as will be
noted below, for believing that the problem is beyond the
ability of educators to solve, at least if they are forced to
deal with it entirely on their own.

Adolescence is a period of revolt, with the child wanting
to become an adult as soon as possible. By the time he has
been in school for eight years, he knows that adults work,
earn money, enjoy sexual freedom, and are masters of their
own fate. The quickest way to achieve adult status, the adolescent then concludes, is to leave school, for as long as
he remains in school, his juvenile status is underscored. This

pull away from the classroom is intensified by the fact that so many adolescents find the teachers dull, the rigid discipline irksome, and the work unpleasant. But this does not necessarily mean that the educators are the ones to blame. The several studies of drop-outs have had one consistent finding. When asked why they left school before graduating, those being questioned inevitably answered that for some time before they quit, they were getting little, if anything, out of school. These youngsters were not acting precipitously. Their decision to leave school merely reflected their desire to trade boring, unproductive activity for something more meaningful to them.

It surely would have been better if school had not bored them, if those last years of school had been more meaningful ones. And maybe the schools are partly at fault that this was so. But the greater share of the blame lies elsewhere —with the community. For the school as it is presently structured is simply not in a position to provide the range of experiences that these young people require. They want, and need, a chance to grow up quickly, not slowly. They need a job, income, and adult relationships. All this the school cannot provide.

Eventually the community will have to face up to these facts. Otherwise it will run the risk of demoralizing a significant proportion of its adolescents. American society, by increasing the opportunities for education, has provided an open sesame for many. But it must also recognize that this is not the answer for all its young citizens. Millions of them need developmental opportunities which the school cannot provide. If they are denied these opportunities, they will become estranged and seek other outlets for their energies, including socially undesirable activities. While adolescent

delinquency can never be totally eliminated, it can be reduced if young people who find school burdensome and
unprofitable are given a chance to work, acquire skills, and
mature in an adult environment.

Two other difficulties have arisen with the lengthening
of the school years. For one thing, girls mature more rapidly
than boys, both physically and emotionally. This fact, although well known to earlier generations of educators, has
sometimes been ignored by their successors. Today's educators are indeed concerned with the psychological facets
of child development. This has led them for many years to
insist that children lock step through the school grades with
other children their own age, rather than with children
younger or older than they. But at the same time they have
paid too little attention to the uneven emotional development of the sexes. In the American coeducational schools
this oversight has had serious consequences. Boys, confined
to the same classrooms as girls maturing more rapidly than
they, face an uneven struggle to keep pace with them. The
teacher, caught between the more sophisticated girls and
the seemingly backward boys, cannot help but find it difficult to evaluate the latter properly. How is the teacher
to allow for differing levels of emotional perception, especially when it comes to judging the work of the student in
literature, history, and the social sciences? It may well be
that the gains from coeducation are substantial. But there is
no denying that the uneven rates at which boys and girls
mature emotionally confronts the high school with a particularly difficult problem, not only in the classroom but in
extracurricular activities as well. One out of every four
women, it must be remembered, is married by the age of
eighteen.

The third difficulty that has arisen involves the tolerance of adolescent males for women teachers. The success of a school depends in large measure on the extent to which the pupils can identify with their teachers. In the absence of such identification, learning becomes difficult, if not impossible. For this reason, the high proportion of women teachers in the secondary school system represents a major additional hurdle for young men. Buffeted and beaten by the pulls and counter-pulls of adolescence, many young men find it extremely hard to profit from classroom instruction when the teacher is a woman. This is the time in their lives when young men are trying to escape from the dominance of their mothers and establish their own male identity. To be under the constant supervision and control of women teachers constitutes yet another difficulty in the path of their development. And while the conflict is much less intense in the case of girls, it also exists for them. They too are in a struggle with their mothers, which is then transferred to their women teachers.

So far, the discussion of the lengthened school years has focused on the high school. But its influence extends beyond that. Although only about half of the young people entering college complete their work and acquire a degree, each decade has seen a higher proportion of the relevant age group enter college. As a result, despite a marked increase in facilities, the pressures for admission on the colleges, especially the more renowned institutions, is now quite intense and will become even more so in the years ahead. This is, in many respects, a healthy sign. But the fact just mentioned, that half who enter college do not finish, suggests that many young people are under misapprehensions about what college has to offer them. This high drop-out rate is due to not just one but a whole series of difficulties.

Years ago college was limited mainly to those who wished to enter certain professions, or to young men and women primarily from families in upper socioeconomic groups to whom college seemed the proper way of spending the late teens and early twenties. More recently, however, the rapid growth of professional, scientific, and managerial positions for which college is a formal requirement or a preferred method of preparation, has led to a broadening of the socioeconomic base from which the colleges draw their students. This also reflects the fact that a great many more families are now in a position to send their children to college for social prestige purposes. Not only will it give their children a chance for a better job, they reason, it will also give them a chance to acquire some polish—and in the case of girls it will probably enable them to marry a young man with a promising future.

For most, if not all, who enter college, their four years of study represent the final transition from adolescence to adulthood. Many are easily subsidized by their parents, business has few promising jobs to offer them at eighteen, and college promises many experiences that will contribute to their growth and maturity even if they have only a modest interest in books and learning.

But despite the fact that many colleges, aware of these factors, seek to create an environment which is as much social as academic, the drop-out rate is high. What they are getting out of their classes does not seem worth the time, money, and effort for many students. They need, and seek, a more adult environment where they can test themselves against more serious challenges than reading books or taking examinations. They are little stimulated by exploring ideas and they have no intention of becoming either scientists or professionals.

In the last few years, a new phenomenon has arisen—an intense scramble by young people to get into one of the preferred colleges. While entrance into these institutions has long been selective, their failure to expand as rapidly as the numbers of young people seeking admission to college has created a crisis, especially along the Atlantic seaboard where the pressure for admission is greatest. As a result, the lives of many adolescents are being complicated and made miserable by the fears of their parents that they will not be accepted by one of the prestige institutions. The youngsters are sent to special schools, given private tutoring, and forced to attend summer school—all in the hope that they will then score high on the entrance examinations.

Most of this pressure is unjustified. It is being exerted by parents who have little understanding of, or interest in intellectual matters, frequently on children whose ability and interests do not run in scholastic channels. It merely reflects the parents' own social aspirations, with little relevance to their children's objective educational needs. Any high school graduate with an adequate preparation can gain admission to a scholastically suitable college. True, many young people will not necessarily be admitted to the college of their choice. But the question arises: Why should they be admitted? Or rather, what does it matter if they go to a college lower on the social and academic scale? Though some may be handicapped by having to attend less stimulating schools, for the great majority it will not matter. If they make the effort, they will get a good education. And if not, whichever institution they attend will make little difference to them.

This unthinking scramble to get into the best colleges is but one of many manifestations of a widespread confusion between the form and substance of education. Lately, under the whiplash of Russian advances in military technology, certain defenders of the American way of life began looking for the reasons why the United States had slipped behind. One reason, they finally decided, was that our school system was grossly inadequate and was failing to provide the quality instruction which the times demanded. Another reason, they concluded, was that young people were not pushing themselves to their full potential. This preoccupation with the Russians coincided with one of these cyclical swings so characteristic of American education, a renewed interest in the "gifted child." As a result, educators began to emphasize "excellence," encouraging gifted young people to concentrate on academic studies rather than on extracurricular activities. Many new scholarships were established and an effort was made to glorify "brain power."

This new orientation has had many beneficial effects, particularly by encouraging gifted students to devote themselves more wholeheartedly to their studies. But there have also been harmful consequences. Grades have always played an important role in the American education system, mainly because there has been no other practical way of evaluating a student's performance. The inherent limitations of a marking system, however, have been sloughed over by pointing to its presumed objectivity. Therefore, when the recent emphasis on academic performance was quickly translated into a stress on better marks, relatively little attention was paid to the danger of equating high marks with educational achievement. The two are not necessarily synonymous. It is a rare student, for example, who is equally talented in mathematics, science, and the humanities. Yet he can hope to win a scholarship to college only if he does well, that is, if he achieves high grades in all the high school subjects he selects. Rather than take courses in those areas in which he is weakest, the student out to beat the examination system will stick largely to the field where his talents lie. But the result is that he fails to obtain a truly balanced college preparation. As long as college admissions and scholarship committees continue to lay primary emphasis on a student's over-all average, this premature and intellectually unwise narrowing of interests will continue. While it is reasonable for educational authorities to insist that young people show a general competence in several fields, it is not reasonable for them to insist on high marks in all fields. It can be assumed a priori that those who achieve a good record across the board, except for a small minority of exceptionally talented youngsters, are more concerned with the trappings than the substance of serious intellectual effort. At the college and graduate school levels, this preoccupation with marks has reached the point of travesty. Many students are taking courses for no other reason than that they are easy and the students can be sure of high grades. At the same time, they avoid more difficult courses which they might well profit from, for fear of adversely affecting their records.

The overemphasis on marks was once even more irrelevant to academic achievement than it is today, for then each local institution was the arbiter of its own standards. There was no way of judging what a high school or college graduate really knew. The diploma which he had earned might represent many different things. He might have studied and mastered a stiff program in science or the humanities. Or he might have done no more than pass a motley of watered-down courses from which he learned little and retained less. But this, to some extent, has now changed. While schools from different regions still have different standards, one positive effect of the recent concern with educational achievement has been a new emphasis on state and national norms. In the future, this should remove some of the ambiguities of the marking system and give students a better insight into their own capabilities. Many a high school valedictorian and many a college straight "A" student, after entering a school where the competition is more intense than he was accustomed to, has had to revise his estimates of his own capabilities.

A BALANCED VIEW

From all that has been said, one might conclude that American education has more weaknesses than strengths and that it faces more challenges than it can successfully meet. But this would miss the point. The public school has merely been given responsibilities which it is not properly equipped to handle. And this has been due to the fact that Americans have expected too much from their schools, that they have tried to make them the unique instrument for the realization of the American dream. Perhaps educational leaders are partly to blame for accepting responsibilities when they lacked adequate resources to meet those responsibilities. But it is not easy in a democracy for any basic institution such as the school to close its eyes to pressing problems, especially if there exists no alternative agency to step into the breach.

The school is the victim of its own success. It did provide the most potent instrument for the Americanization of millions of immigrant children. It did enable many young people, by providing them with free education through the high school level, to make a more satisfying vocational choice ultimately. And it did help many more young people to make up for the deficiencies and shortcomings of their family and social environment.

Admittedly, lengthening of the school years has brought new problems—problems which only community action can remedy. A few have already been mentioned. One could also cite the inadequate services provided children from disadvantaged families, the shortage and insufficient training of faculties and staffs, the failure to devise appropriate curricula for pupils with modest intellectual capacity and limited motivation. Still, one fact must be kept in mind. No matter how many problems still await solution, no matter how many new problems the schools will have to cope with in the decades ahead, schools have provided the open sesame for a significant proportion of citizens —a larger proportion by far than in any other country. The shortcomings which still exist in our educational system should not obscure this major accomplishment.

* VII

LIFE PLANS

The foregoing chapters have shown how ideology and reality in the United States have reinforced each other to create a favorable environment for the improvement of youth. Parents assume that it will be possible for their children to live a better life than they did, and their offspring in turn grow up assuming that they will be able to improve the circumstances which characterized the lives of their parents. Beyond the immediate family, the community as a whole is committed by belief and deed to establishing and strengthening those institutions that will contribute to this end.

What is sometimes overlooked, however, is the fact that the outcome—whether children will in fact lead a life noticeably better than that of their parents—depends to a large extent on the values and goals of youth and that these values and goals will determine how effectively young people will make use of their capabilities.

Folklore holds that all Americans would like to get to the top, that every boy would like to be President. Yet the proof of this is lacking. To most of its native-born citizens, and more particularly to most of the immigrants who came to its shores, the United States offered an opportunity to get ahead simply by standing still. The very thrust of westward expansion and the resulting economic prosperity have produced a more or less steady rise in living standards since the colonial period. At the same time there have been striking gains in religious and political freedom. Binding the two together and in part the result of them has been the remarkable fluidity of social classes, which has meant that no person has had to resign himself to permanent membership in a lower class. The uniqueness of this American situation was suggested by one of our earlier monographs, *European Impressions of the American Worker*, and it is documented more extensively in our forthcoming volume, *The American Worker in the Twentieth Century*.

In short, every American could, with only a moderate effort, get on the escalator of rising material benefits. If he decided that he wished to ascend more rapidly, as many in each generation did, he could simply run up the moving stairs. If he did not slip, he could make a very speedy ascent.

For every young man three decisions largely determine the success of his efforts to give shape and meaning to his life. The first is his choice of a career, including the antecedent decisions with respect to education. The second is his choice of a program to fulfill his military commitment. The third is his choice of a marital partner. This is not to ignore the fact that a young person's margins of freedom may be limited and, in many instances, may be quite narrow. Yet they are relatively greater in American society than in any other.

A person's values, the mainspring of his actions, are much more than simply the product of his own struggle for identity and independence. They are also the outgrowth of his cumulative experience since infancy. With puberty and adolescence, a youth gains more freedom for self-expression and self-determination, but he is still forced to remain within the grooves cut earlier. In the shaping of a young person's values, the influence of parents and peers is likely to be greater than the searchings of the individual himself. And yet the scope for individual choice is substantial.

The young person's emerging values and goals provide important anchors that enable him slowly to give up his fantasies of adulthood and seek to orient his efforts in a more realistic direction. In the event that he has rather modest goals for himself, a reflection of lack of stimulation and help from his parents and from others in his immediate environment, or else of unresolved emotional conflict, the consequence may be lack of motivation. This will result in an underdevelopment of his potentialities and capacities, involving among other things a failure to utilize effectively the opportunities which exist in the larger environment.

For a person to be successful later in life, he requires while still young a strong spiritual foundation—that is, the nourishment of certain fundamental values and a setting of challenging goals. Yet if his parents cannot provide him with the proper stimulation or if he himself cannot resolve his emotional conflicts, a young person may fail to utilize his full potential. Or it may happen that the parents make themselves appear so successful to the youngster that he fears he can never match their accomplishments and so sets himself a less than fully challenging goal. Hence the expression arises, "Three generations from riches to rags."

Of the three types of decision which a young man must make—occupational, military, and marital—the first provides him with the most direct opportunity to realize his values and goals. For the work that a man does usurps such a large part of his time and energies that it inevitably shapes his life off the job too. Here deliberate choice—the objective assessment of the advantages and disadvantages of various alternatives—is possible to a much larger extent than in the other two areas. In regard to military service, the margins for individual maneuver are relatively narrow, and in the event of a national emergency may all but disappear. And in the case of marital choice, emotional and instinctual pressures may radically reduce the area of rational discretion.

OCCUPATIONAL CHOICE

In 1951, we published the results of an exploratory study, *Occupational Choice: An Approach to a General Theory*. The following draws heavily from this research.

A person's occupational choice is not a one-time decision but the cumulative result of many decisions over time. These decisions reinforce each other until the occupational path open to an individual has been narrowly delineated. The facts that one is young only once, that one goes to school only once, and that one can prepare for only one profession at a time effectively limits the alternatives open to an individual at various stages of his life. But certain alternatives exist nonetheless. It is well, therefore, to point out the framework in which these alternatives are weighed.

Even very young children will tell you what they want to be when they grow up. Usually it is some exciting, dramatic occupation, such as aviator, soldier, or nurse. Without having to worry about how practical such dreams are, young children can easily give their fantasy full reign. But even fantasy can be the first step in the long, tortuous process of crystalizing one's thinking about the kind of work one would like eventually to do. A four-year-old girl, if asked whether she would like one day to be a physician, may reply that this is not possible. Only men, not women, are doctors, she may tell you. Faulty as this judgment is, it shows that the four-year-old is already making important distinctions about the world of work and the jobs appropriate to each sex.

Around the age of eleven, when young people begin to recognize for the first time that sooner or later they will have to choose the type of work they would like to do later in life, the process of occupational choice enters a new stage. First the young person chooses a field of study that interests him; then, as he nears the end of high school, he tries to match an occupation with his academic interests. This is the transition from tentative to realistic choice, from exploration to crystallization.

The very nature of the educational system constantly forces a young person to choose among various alternatives —which high school to enter, what course to pursue, whether or not to apply to college, what major to select, whether or not to enter professional or graduate school. And each decision reduces the alternatives open to him.

This is the complex process of choosing an occupation, which begins in early childhood and continues for almost twenty years. During the last ten years, the young person himself is directly involved in making choices, even if these consist of no more than following the line of least resistance.

It is a rare youngster indeed who experiences little or no difficulty in resolving the problem of occupational choice. No matter how narrow the areas of discretion may be, the number of options available to him is considerable, whether he be a diligent student or a sluggish one, whether he come from an affluent home or a low-income family. That he will reach the age of partial discretion—puberty or adolescence—so deeply committed to one career goal that he has no doubts about it is unlikely. Some may be strongly drawn to certain fields, but even they are likely to consider various alternatives. More typically, however, young people do not feel a powerful pull in any direction. Instead, they find it difficult to translate their academic interests into meaningful careers. Contrary to what many parents and counselors think, a student who does well in science will not necessarily be happy as a doctor, nor will one who does well in history necessarily be happy as a teacher.

At the same time, the failure of parents and counselors to understand the process of occupational choice often makes the decisions of youngsters more difficult. Many parents push their children to decide on a career long before they are intellectually and emotionally capable of doing so. If this pressure is great enough, the result may well be an over-anxious, confused, or prematurely committed child. But the opposite danger also exists. Some children are not pushed enough. At key stages in their life, when they should make important career decisions, they may simply ignore the problem so that, when they are finally ready to leave school, they are without definite career plans. While they will sooner or later find jobs, they may not be the ones that will satisfy them, and they may spend several years or longer looking for the type of work that will prove suitable to them. Their failure to think seriously about the future probably prevented them from getting very much out of school, and this in turn probably made a satisfactory occupational adjustment later on more difficult.

There is another danger. Young people may commit themselves to a particular career goal before they have had an adequate opportunity to test the depth of their interest or the strength of their capability. By the time they discover what their true interests or strengths are, however, it may well be too late for them to change their career plans and they may wind up dissatisfied with their work. Such a premature commitment is likeliest to occur in fields which require long years of study and preparation.

The problem of choosing a career, difficult as it may be, can become even more complicated when a young person must also decide how he will fit his military commitments into his career plans. To this second major area of decision making, we now turn.

COMPULSORY MILITARY SERVICE

Since 1940, approximately 25 million men have served in the armed forces. Throughout most of these two decades, except for one brief period in 1947–48, the great bulk of these men have entered the military service because of the draft. But the significance of this for the lives of young people has not been fully appreciated. Apparently our anti-militaristic tradition has led the American public to view the armed forces as something apart from the rest of its life, except in war or in time of national emergency. Men enlist or are drafted, they serve for two, three, or four years, and then, except for a small number who decide to make armed services a career, they return to civilian life and quickly turn their backs on their military experience.

In recent years a new factor has been added. Young men coming of draft age are no longer certain that they will have to serve. While the numbers deferred or exempted for various reasons have always been larger in the United States than among our allies, until recently about seven out of every ten young men eventually served in some capacity. But currently the ratio is dropping, and, unless the international situation should worsen perceptibly or the entire system of military manpower procurement be altered, the proportion of young men called to duty may decline to one out of two in the eligible age group and, later in the decade to only one out of three. The numbers of young men coming of draft age are very much larger than those required to fill the needs of the armed services, particularly in light of the services' strenuous efforts to build up a career force.

Military service, instead of being an obligation which all young men recognize, has become more and more of a gamble in which certain players hold marked cards. For instance those who go on with their studies, the more intelligent and the more well-to-do, are deferred until their studies have been completed. While they are technically subject to call until they are thirty-five, most of them will probably not see service because, among other reasons, the armed services prefer younger men. There are also many young men who marry early. They, too, while technically subject to call, are not generally being inducted. And finally, there are the ever-increasing proportions of each age group who are being turned down because, in the opinion of the armed services, they do not possess the intellectual ability, the physical strength, the emotional stability, or the moral integrity to make good servicemen. Able to pick from a more-than-adequate pool, the armed services have steadily raised their standards of acceptability.

While young men are subject to service under an act entitled Universal Military Training and Service, each year sees the concept of universality further violated. Admittedly, the country faces a difficult problem in working out a sound solution. The armed forces must be able to secure the num-

ber of men that Congress has authorized, either by enlist-
ment or through Selective Service. Since enlistments are
insufficient to supply the armed services with all the manpower they need, recourse to the draft is unavoidable. But
the supply of eligible young men is increasing far in excess
of the numbers required, with the result that more and more
young men will not be called upon to serve.

Until the Berlin crisis in the fall of 1961, only an occa-
sional congressman or student of public affairs had expressed
concern about the implication of a system of military manpower procurement that deviates increasingly from the cri-
terion of universality. The armed forces were getting the
men they needed; the Selective Service system continued
in business, and most individuals chose the time they would
serve, whether in the army, air force, navy, or marine corps.
Sometimes they even chose the type of duty they would
perform. Under such circumstances, it was not surprising
that the critics were few and that their criticism failed to
evoke a large-scale and favorable response. Even today the
public accepts the fact that the country requires sizable
military forces to halt the expansion of international com-
munism and it is apparently willing to accept the deviation
from universality in favor of a practical resolution to an
admittedly difficult predicament, in which the armed forces
need some but not all of the men eligible to serve.

But it may well be that the public does not fully realize
the implications of acquiescing to the present arrangements,
which stem largely from the Department of Defense and
interested congressional committees.

The last time the Universal Military Training and Service Act was extended, in 1959, Congress was unwilling to

authorize, as one congressman suggested, a detailed evaluation of the complex problem of military manpower needs and requirements. Rather than open Pandora's box, the lawmakers extended the old act as quickly and unobtrusively as possible.

The fact that military manpower policy has been left to the interested few and has not caught the attention of the larger public goes far to explain why so little thought has been given to the consequences of a system that encourages young people to "play the odds." Currently, the young man who "gets caught" and who serves for two or more years on active duty is likely to consider himself a "sucker," for that is how his friends who escape military service regard him. The uncertainty that surrounds a man's obligation to serve makes it more difficult for him to plan intelligently when to serve and in what capacity. And it makes it much more difficult for those who eventually do serve to consider their assignments and responsibilities constructively—to do their best and to try to profit as much as possible from their experience. They are much more likely to consider themselves as unfortunate "victims of the system," who are "serving time." Military service, they are convinced, has little if anything to contribute to their development. As a result, their major objective is to find a good assignment, which means an easy assignment, preferably one where passes are frequent.

In point of fact, the armed services have made and are continuing to make a major contribution to the development of a great many young men on a great many different fronts —in terms of education, occupation, health, social skills, and general personal development. Indicative of the American public's attitude toward military service is the fact that this wide impact of the armed services on youth has largely gone unnoticed.

We cannot here do justice to the full range of this impact, but it may be helpful to suggest within the general theme of this book on the improvement of youth some of the principal lines of influence which the armed forces exert.

There is little question but that the occupational horizons of many young men are considerably expanded as a result of their military service. Through travel, they have an opportunity to learn about many types of work which are unknown in their home communities. They also can learn about job opportunities from their barrackmates and officers. Moreover, they are encouraged to pursue their education on off-duty hours, and this opens areas of potential employment for which they may not have been qualified previously. And most importantly, they are able to secure training in such skilled occupations as electronics, medicine, communications, and mechanics, many of which have direct counterparts in civilian life. Many who acquired the elements of a skill while on active duty are later able to develop a satisfactory civilian career on this foundation.

Those who became entitled to veteran's benefits through their service—and that covers most of the men who have served since 1940—have had new and expanded opportunities for education and training. They were frequently able to reconsider their occupational choices. With tuition and maintenance assured for two, three, or even four years, they could even look forward to entering a scientific, professional, or skilled occupation which previously would have been beyond their reach, though not necessarily beyond their ambition or capacity.

The armed services have also done much to improve the physical health and emotional stability of American youth by introducing millions of them to proper regimens of diet and personal hygiene, acquainting them with the potentialities of modern medicine and dentistry, and providing them with a heterogeneous social environment where they were challenged and encouraged to get along with individuals from diverse backgrounds.

In this connection it is well to emphasize that outstanding progress on the racial front has occurred as a result of the final desegregation of the armed services during the early 1950s. In this important sector of our national life, Negroes have a pilot model of an environment in which every form of legal discrimination has been eliminated. And equally, if not more important, millions of young white men have learned to live with Negroes in every relationship—as superiors, equals, subordinates. There has been no more forceful lesson in race relations than when white boys from the deep South learned through personal experience that Negroes were capable of command, that they were often skilled and talented, and that their response to danger, challenge, or opportunity was not greatly different from their own.

While it has been relatively easy to identify many positive contributions the armed services have made to the improvement of American youth, the fact that the country must still make use of Selective Service to fill its armed ranks is incontestable. Most young Americans look upon active military duty with distaste. Such an attitude derives first, from the national ethos that in times of peace any forced restriction of individual freedom is bad; next, from the belief that the years that a man spends in uniform are wasted and will set him back in his career; lastly, from the widespread feeling that large-scale forces are unnecessary in an age of atomic weapons.

Whatever the rationale, the simple fact remains that young men are growing up without any sense of obligation to serve in the armed forces. As they approach the end of high school, many confront the situation for the first time. But many others who are on their way to college and graduate school can push the issue far into the future. Although much foolishness has been written about the American prisoners of war in Korea who went over to the enemy, it cannot be gainsaid that in Korea, as in World War II, a disturbingly high percentage of the men on active duty had little perception of the relationship between the sacrifices they were asked to make and the predicament of their country. They had grown up without being conditioned to the necessity of military service—in fact many had been negatively conditioned by the widespread pacifist agitation prior to World War II. There is a disturbing parallel in the current situation where once again the anticipation of eventual military service is not part of the positive life planning of most young men. They know that they may have to serve but they hope not to.

The fact that in Korea a few prisoners went over to the enemy and many more collapsed to a point where they would not struggle to stay alive does not bespeak, as some military psychiatrists have argued, a collapse in the moral fiber of American youth. Instead it bespeaks serious shortcomings in the education which these men received, both in civilian life and in the military; more particularly, it bespeaks the failure of the military command structure after the men were taken prisoner. In view of the half-hearted support which the fighting men received from the home front it can even be argued that the small number who defected is testimony to the character of American youth.

Shifting the focus from past to future, it is not possible to be sanguine. Despite the appalling seriousness of the power struggle in which this country is currently engaged, most young men grow up without any understanding of military obligation, with the consequence that if and when they are called to duty, they view it as an imposition, an annoyance, or a stroke of bad luck that they were caught while so many others escaped.

To make matters worse, Congress provided an option in 1955 for a considerable number of young men, enabling them to discharge their military obligation by serving for six months on active military and then five and a half years in the active reserve. These men are usually set apart and trained separately in the army; and all too many of them are assigned to reserve units characterized by inadequate leadership, equipment, and training. As a result, they become even more disillusioned with the military. They talk loosely about the waste they see in their training and service and thereby reenforce the negative attitudes of others.

There are many inherent difficulties in operating a large-scale reserve system effectively—difficulties stemming from lack of funds, equipment, leadership, and time. Many reserve units have succeeded in surmounting these very real difficulties, but many more have not.

There are many other ramifications of compulsory military service that could be explored, but the preceding summary discussion should highlight the crucial issue: the necessity to reevaluate the system and to refashion it in such a manner that it contributes as much as possible to the security of the nation and the welfare of the individual. Nothing is more dangerous, especially for a democracy, than to permit basic military manpower policy to escape continuing and penetrating public discussion. Only if the public understands why demands are being made on it can it be motivated to respond effectively. For a democracy to permit and encourage its young men to grow up viewing military service as a burden to be avoided is an invitation to national disaster.

The call-up of reservists incident to the Berlin crisis of 1961 revealed still another order of difficulty with the system. Despite the widespread criticism of the inequities that occurred during the Korean hostilities when men who had never served were permitted to remain in their civilian pursuits while veterans who had not been actively participating in a reserve program were called back to active duty to serve a second time, and despite the effort of the 1955 Reserve Act to prevent a repetition of such inequities, the recent call-up caught a considerable number of individuals with prior service—some few with two previous stints—while many others in the active reserve without prior extended duty but in pay status were not ordered to active duty. The complaints have reached such a high pitch that some corrective action is likely.

EARLY MARRIAGE

While at first it may be difficult to see any logical connection between compulsory military service and the age at which young people marry, a moment's reflection should make clear that there are many. Most obviously, an unknown but probably sizable number of young men are encouraged to marry, to escape military service by becoming fathers. Moreover, whether a young man goes into service or not will determine whether he will be around during the next two to four years, and this in turn may encourage him to reach a quicker decision about a young woman whom he has started to court. In turn, his impending removal from the scene may lead the young woman to press the matter to a successful conclusion before he gets away.

The fact that military pay represents for many young men their first steady, if modest, income encourages many of them to marry, for they also take into account that their wives will receive a special allowance.

Nor can one overlook the fear of loneliness in the hearts of many who are wrenched away from their familiar surroundings for the first time in their lives. A considerable number of young men who enter the army single marry during the course of their military service, often in a desperate effort to find some substitute for what they had to leave behind.

These are but a few of the connections between military service and early marriage. While it would be possible to identify factors that tend to delay rather than hasten marriage, on the balance it seems that military service is one of the forces in American society today making for early nuptials.

At present, about one quarter of all young women are married before the age of eighteen and more than half are married before they are twenty-one. This represents the lowest average age of marriage in the nation's history, and one of the lowest, if not the lowest, of any modern industrial society.

Historically, the very wealthy and improvident poor married early—and for largely the same reason. Money was no barrier, for the rich because they had all they needed; for the poor because they lived only for the moment without regard to the future. In recent decades, the high level of employment has made it possible for young people, even for those without advanced education or special skill, to find jobs where they could earn from the start as much as $60 a week, and before long, even more. This means that a young couple can look forward to a combined income of over $6,000 a year—more than enough to set up and run a home. Able to support themselves, many young couples see no reason even to ask their parents' consent. If their parents object to such an early marriage the young couple can take care of themselves.

Early marriages today occur among a large number of college students as well as among a small number of high school students. Among the college group there are many who require and receive continuing support from their parents. When the parents are unable or unwilling to help, or where the young people prefer not to ask them, the wife frequently drops out of school and goes to work while the young man continues his studies. Among graduate students, it is understood that a wife can underwrite a man's studies just as effectively—and perhaps even more so—than a graduate scholarship or fellowship.

There is no single or simple explanation for the trend toward early marriage. It has resulted from the confluence of a great many forces, including the puritanical view of most Americans towards sexual relations outside of matrimony, the acceleration in sexual maturation through improved dietary and living conditions, the increasingly heterosexual nature of our educational and recreational facilities which throw boys and girls together from puberty on, the uncertainties of military service which make many young people fear the consequences of prolonged separation, and the relaxed attitudes of young people about what the future holds in store for them. They are sure that they will find jobs and discharge their responsibilities, including the support of a family, the size of which will be under their control.

There is a close relationship between the changing attitudes of Americans, already sketched, towards work and the increased frequency of early marriage. One of the major reasons that men postponed marriage in earlier decades was their desire to be well-set in their careers before assuming responsibility for a wife and children. Much has changed. As argued in the last chapter, the nonwork areas of life have grown in importance over the work areas. In *The Nation's Children*, Moses Abramovitz pointed out that in recent years professionally trained persons no longer have to accumulate considerable capital to get started in their careers. What they need is supplied them by the organizations, profit or nonprofit, for which they work. Nor must one overlook the fact that one of the concomitants of a growing affluence is the even larger number of young people who have some money of their own—which they have been given or which they have been able to save.

For these and other reasons, the young man no longer faces a sharp choice—wife or career. He is often in a position to have both, as shown by the large number of young physicians who marry while still in medical school and the much larger number who marry before completing their internship and residency training.

Until now, the emphasis has been on the male because young women have always been interested in marrying early, but have usually had to wait until their young men were in a position to do so. For most young women see their fulfilment in marriage and children.

This last point helps to explain not only why young people marry early but also why many of them have children shortly afterward. In fact, many marriages take place because a child is on the way. But the more typical pattern is for a young couple to start their family shortly after they are married. This is, at first glance, not easy to understand in a society where knowledge of contraception is widespread. The explanation must be sought in the social pressures which produce not only early marriage but also early family formation.

Young people are sensitive to the behavior of their peers. They hesitate to deviate. When they find many of their friends marrying early, they are strongly impelled to do likewise. When a college junior finds that her three best friends have dropped out of school during the summer because they married, this may be enough to tip the scales in favor of her accepting a proposal which, up to that point, she has been uncertain about. She does not want to return to school alone and face the task of developing a whole new set of friends. And young men also become restive when they notice that the most attractive girls are being taken out of circulation.

The same competitive pressures operate with respect to children. When their friends have a child every year and a half or every two years, most young couples will indeed feel pressure to do likewise. Moreover, they are likely to be impressed with the conventional wisdom that young parents make the best parents.

Many thoughtful people, professionals and laymen, have questioned the soundness of early marriage. One expert, concerned about the high rate of divorce among young couples, has remarked that today the first marriage is really a trial marriage. Despite these strictures there is every reason to expect the present trend to continue, and if the level of employment remains high it is likely that the average age of marriage may drop even lower.

There is one important consequence of the present pattern that has not been fully appreciated—its influence on the career choices and occupational behavior of young men of high ability. Even in those instances where the young wife is willing to see her husband through graduate school she is not likely to want to support her husband after he has completed his degree. As soon as he has his course work behind him, she is likely to press him to start their family, for this is the pattern of the day. And the young man at the beginning of his career may then make his job decisions in light of his growing family responsibilities. He will be much more interested in current income than in future prospects, in fringe benefits than in opportunities to broaden and deepen his skills. Moreover, his mobility will be limited. He will have to weigh job offers not only in terms of what they might contribute to his future but also their desirability from the viewpoint of locating his family.

The overriding fact is that at the very outset of his career the young husband and particularly the young father must pay more attention to the immediate needs of his family than to his future career. He must be concerned with exploiting what he already knows rather than with accumulating additional knowledge so that he can perform in the future on a higher level of competence.

While it is reasonable to question whether young people whose life experience has been limited to attending school have acquired the requisite maturity to make a good marital choice, or whether on balance it is desirable for a couple to marry even though they must be supported for several years by their parents, there is little likelihood that the present pattern will change. And as far as the majority of young people are concerned, the advantages and disadvantages of this new pattern may balance.

The disadvantages may be more social than individual. While early marriage may yield many satisfactions to those personally involved, a society cannot ignore the fact that it may interrupt the higher education of many able young women and may interfere with the occupational development of many able young men. These untoward results, however, stem more from young couples' having children early than from their marrying early.

Whether the link between the two—early marriage and early family formation—will continue as in the recent past, will depend on a great many factors, including the extent to which young men and women in the future question the wisdom of tying themselves down early in their married life. But as long as the family and children continue to furnish young people their major gratification, it will be only the exceptional individual who stands against the trend and concentrates during his twenties on advancing his education and getting a good start in his career.

VIII

EXPANDING HORIZONS

One outstanding characteristic of American society has been the breadth of its commitment to equality of opportunity. All sorts of people, regardless of their religious, educational, or cultural backgrounds, have been welcomed to this country and given an opportunity to participate in its growth. Such opportunities have not been limited to the children of the native born but have included the children of the immigrant as well. All have had access to broadened opportunity.

For two important groups, however, American democracy has failed to fulfill its promise—for women and for Negroes. While educational opportunities for women were always much greater in this country than in Europe, it was not until World War II that married women found a place in the job market. As for Negroes, the current struggle over civil rights, both in the North and in the South, bears witness to the gap which still exists between the promise of American democracy and the reality of their position. Still, the Negro, within recent decades and particularly since World War II, has begun to share more fully in American life. The unique position of women and Negroes— their lag behind other groups in reaping the benefits of American democracy and their recent strides forward toward greater equality, particularly in the world of work—

justifies singling them out and dealing with them as a special case.

It is the ideas and ideals of the older generation that become the guideposts for directing the young; these ideas and ideals usually reflect the circumstances under which the older generation grew up. Hence, in a period of rapid, almost revolutionary change, a serious gap is likely to develop. The experience of the parents no longer fits the needs of their children. And the same is true of others who act as advisors to the young: teachers, guidance counselors, and youth workers. This means that young people growing up in a world of rapid change have an additional hurdle to surmount. The advice they receive will often reflect conditions that are fast disappearing.

It is a problem not only of attitudes but also of institutions. Institutions by their very nature reflect the prevailing views as to the appropriateness of things. When circumstances force a change in these views, established institutions are likely to lag behind. It has taken considerable time, for example, for our political institutions to adjust to the fact that women now have the right to vote in national elections. Similarly, many landlords have been slow to perceive that in a period of aggressive desegregation it makes little sense to rent to an African Negro but not to an American one.

This chapter will explore changing attitudes toward women and Negroes, emphasizing the problems which young people are likely to face in trying to get their bearings, when established patterns of life are dissolving and the outline of the new one can only be dimly perceived.

WOMEN AND WORK

At the very time that the role of work in American society is losing some of its significance in the life of men, the country is witnessing a radical change in the employment of married women. Since the beginning of World War II, the proportion of married women in the labor force has expanded rapidly, and even the current high figures give no evidence that a ceiling has been reached. At the present time, of the almost thirty million women who work for wages during the course of a year approximately twenty million are married. If present trends continue, the typical pattern of a woman's life may well be that she will remain in school until she marries, between the ages of eighteen and twenty-two; that she will have two or three children during the first decade of her married life; that she will enter the labor market in her early thirties when her youngest child is ready for school; and that she will work part or full time for the next twenty-five or thirty years, until she is eligible for social security.

The National Manpower Council, in its comprehensive study of *Womanpower* (1957), identified the many forces that played a part in bringing about this "revolution," which inevitably is having an important impact not only on the women themselves, but also on their husbands and children and on the functioning of the family and society.

Many older women who today hold down jobs grew up in communities where no married women, except those who had been widowed and left without means, or were otherwise disadvantaged by being immigrants or Negroes, were likely to work. Yet despite the absence of models, millions of older married women are working today. This fact should serve as a reminder of the potency of social forces to alter fundamental behavior patterns and should further serve as a warning that the present pattern is also subject to change. The fact that the mothers of many young women growing up today work out of the home yields only a presumption, not a guarantee, that their daughters will do likewise.

People with problems commonly believe that their circumstances are unique. Hence many women believe that the conflicts between family and career that they face trouble their sex alone, that men do not have the same conflicts. But, as the last chapter revealed, many men do in fact face very real counter-pulls between their work and their family. And the resolution which they make, more often than not, is in favor of their families. Yet one cannot deny that a young woman faces distinctive problems with respect to work, problems deriving specifically from her sexual-social role. While significant changes have taken place, and will continue to take place, in the help and assistance that wives, especially working wives, receive from their husbands in caring for the children and in running the household, the fact remains that women face certain demands, especially in the bearing of children and in their care during the first years, that they alone can fulfill.

This being so, most young women grow up with the expectation that their primary role will be as wife and mother —taking care of their husbands, running the household, and, for the most part, rearing the children. As a practical matter, most young women realize that these domestic activities are likely to usurp all their energies, especially during the years when the children are young. Small wonder, therefore, that only a minority of young women grow up making careful vocational plans.

The evidence indicates that young women are much less concerned than young men about developing their intellectual abilities to the full—witness the much smaller proportion who complete college (about one woman to every two men) despite the fact that more girls than boys graduate from high school. Equally revealing is the smaller percentage of high school girls who pursue an academic course and the very small number of women college graduates who undertake graduate work and earn their masters' or doctorate degrees, the field of education excepted.

There are two possible explanations for these facts. Either young women are not aware of the changes taking place in the work pattern of married women or, despite their awareness, they still have little interest in preparing for or pursuing a career. Possibly both are true.

The young learn about the world from their parents, teachers, and friends and, when they are somewhat older, through their own direct experience. But during puberty and adolescence their view of the world of work will be shaped mostly by what they learn at home and at school. And young girls undoubtedly hear much about the barriers that women face in the job market.

Mothers and teachers who themselves experienced major difficulties in finding suitable employment and in obtaining fair treatment probably are still responding to their own experience rather than objectively appraising the current situation, or even more important, imaginatively projecting what the future holds for their children and pupils.

For these and other reasons, many young women growing up today ignore the changing pattern of women's work and the new opportunities that have opened up. They complete college having majored in English or modern languages without giving serious consideration to how they will earn their livelihood. In fact, there are well-known women's colleges that fail to provide their students with occupational guidance until a few weeks before graduation. Many superior women college graduates, unable to find employment where they can use their education, turn desperately to secretarial school after their graduation from college.

But it would be naïve to assume that order can be brought out of the present confusion simply by providing better guidance for young women during their formative years in school. There are certain facts that cannot be ignored. By seventeen or eighteen the average young woman is primarily interested in expanding her acquaintance with young men—if she is not already engaged—with an aim of eventually choosing a husband. Everything else is secondary, and for good reason. Whether she prepares herself for one kind of job or another, whether she continues in school or not, whether she accepts a position during the summer or not, all of these decisions are minor in comparison with her principal concern, her progress in finding the right man. Women's colleges such as Barnard in New York City are inundated with applications from metropolitan area residents who have been attending out-of-town and out-of-state colleges and who now want to transfer in order to be close to their boyfriends, or who believe that they will have a better chance of finding boyfriends on their home grounds. And there are many coeducational colleges that attract girl students because of the marital, rather than educational, opportunities that they offer. For the young woman instinctively understands that her marital decision will do more to shape the structure of her future life than any educational or occupational plan that she might have.

In fact, even if she were able to ignore the problem of marriage, it would still be difficult for her to formulate a sound occupational plan. There are not many careers that she can enter, only to leave shortly afterward for a decade or more while she raises her children, then to reenter in her thirties when her time and traveling ability are still severely limited.

The American economy, being highly competitive, does not make special allowances for the needs of married women who want to pursue seriously both a career as a wife and mother and as a professional or office worker. She can work part or full time when she is ready to do so, but seldom at a level commensurate with her education and skills (especially in the case of the college graduate) and seldom under conditions where she can expand her competence and improve her position—without straining herself beyond her physical and emotional limits. For the married woman, even when all of her children are in school, still has many responsibilities at home.

Young women growing up today face an inherently difficult problem. If they continue to turn away from any serious consideration of how to make the best use of the educational and occupational opportunities opening up for them, they will unnecessarily limit their future career options. As we have noted, they will have, on the average, as much as three decades of possible work experience. But if, on the other hand, they address themselves seriously to the question of a career outside of the home, that is, if they approach the problem of occupational choice on the same terms as men, they face a host of other difficulties. To mention only a few: How are they going to complete their formal education, especially if it requires that they remain in school until they are twenty-five, and at the same time marry and start their families at an early age? How, after completing their studies, will they be able to work, particularly full time when, the demands on them as homemakers will be at a maximum? If they decide, as so many do, to concentrate on their household tasks when their children are young, how can they hope to stay abreast of developments in their field? And what opportunities will they have to bring their knowledge up to date concerning job opportunities available to them when, finally, they are ready to return to work?

Clearly these are difficult questions to answer. A small minority of women, if they are fortunate enough to have a well-to-do father or husband, may be able to hire someone to help with the household tasks, thus enabling them to cope with the simultaneous demands of home and career. And some may be fortunate or foresightful enough to develop a speciality that does not require them to spend too much time on the job. Some professional women can pursue an editorial career largely at home and certain psychoanalysts can see patients between the hours of 10 A.M. and 4 P.M. in their offices at home. But these are exceptions.

However, it may yet turn out that many of the problems that have been sketched above will have a greater poignancy for social scientists concerned about the waste of human resources than for the greater number of American women. Judging from current behavior, the latter may be reasonably satisfied with the way things are. They can earn supplemental incomes without investing heavily in their jobs.

Yet even the noncareer-woman faces serious difficulties. As suggested earlier, a married woman, even one with a wide range of skills, cannot always find a job in her home community. Much depends on the size of the labor supply, the nature of local industry, and tradition. Even if jobs are available, she may have to settle for one which makes only limited demands on her knowledge and experience.

It is easier to reconstruct what has happened than it is to foretell the shape of things to come. Urbanization, smaller families, easier housekeeping, fewer jobs that require brawn, the social emancipation of women, all these provided the favorable background for the revolutionary change that World War II, in creating a demand for married women to fill jobs essential to the war effort, brought about. Finding work a welcome relief after an often too narrowly circumscribed home life, finding the additional income useful in balancing an expanding budget, and finding it possible to shift some of the conventional household duties to husbands and children, it was not too surprising that a great many married women remained in the labor market at the end of World War II. The revolution turned out to be permanent; thereafter married women had a place in the labor market.

But the situation remains cloudy. The more a woman cares about the full development of her intellectual and occupational potentials, the more difficult it becomes for her to find a satisfactory solution. There are limits to what she can do on her own, even with the full cooperation of her husband and of her children. Much depends on whether the economy needs her, and whether employers, educational authorities, and other influential groups in the country will make special efforts to help her develop and use her potential skills. World War II marked a breakthrough for many women who sought salaried employment. Their complete acceptance and full utilization, however, is still largely in the future. Whether it comes sooner, or later, or is indefinitely delayed, depends on how ingeniously our society can develop new ways of utilizing the latent talent to help solve the important, imminent needs of the nation.

Regrettably, many well-endowed young women face continuing confusion, dissatisfaction, and frustration in seeking a solution to a problem that, basically, lies beyond their power to solve. But even if the school, the economy, and society at large imaginatively support, rather than interfere with, their search for a solution, most women would still face a dilemma. No matter what new social arrangements are made, women will always have special responsibility for rearing the young. And to a greater or lesser degree, this will always interfere with their careers. For them, even more than for men, compromise is essential.

The basic dilemma elaborated above particularly besets that small group of women who are less concerned with additional income than with finding an outlet for their energies, commensurate with their education and potential. These women now face large difficulties in trying to span the two worlds of home and job. If the conventional hours of work should be reduced to thirty-two or less, as they well might be over the next decade or so, the difficulties for these women will be eased. Colleges and universities, for their part, are beginning to deal more realistically with the needs of the educated, mature woman seeking to return to work. Moreover, when industry is particularly hard pressed for trained people, it is sometimes willing to make major concessions to the needs of married women in its hiring, training, and promotion policies, as well as in its hours of work, overtime, and scheduling of vacations. But the fact remains that even in the 1950s, a decade characterized by a short supply of scientific and technically trained personnel, employers were willing to make relatively only a few adjustments along these lines. Unless the unexpected occurs, the 1960s are not likely, because of the much larger number of young people entering the labor market, to see further concessions to the needs of married women.

RACIAL AND ETHNIC MINORITIES

It is not easy to define a minority group. Women, for example, although a majority of the total population, are a minority in the labor market, where they have long been subject to serious discrimination in terms of the jobs open to them, the wages paid them, and, more particularly, the training available to them.

Similar difficulties arise in defining social, ethnic, and religious minorities. The width of the lens largely determines the picture that emerges. In the United States as a whole, Catholics are clearly a minority. But in Rhode Island, or even New York City, Catholics comprise the majority. In New York County, none of the State Supreme Court Justices are Protestants of Anglo-Saxon extraction, an example of discrimination against a minority that is frequently overlooked. There is no state south of the Mason and Dixon line which does not have at least one county where the Negroes comprise the majority. And there are several counties in Texas where Mexican-Americans are the most numerous group.

There is no need to belabor the point. In a country of continental dimensions, minority group status depends on where you are and who you are. There are in this country literally thousands of minority groups, each with special advantages and disadvantages. A Jew may not be admitted to a certain exclusive country club but he does have a preferred chance of succeeding in the garment industry. And a person over sixty-five may find certain jobs closed to him, but he can still count on Social Security and tax benefits.

There is a minority, however, that has few of the advantages but many of the disadvantages. It is a minority, moreover, made conspicuous by the color of its skin. Farmers can move to the city; old people die; men can change their religions—but except for a very small number who are able and willing to pass over into the white community, Negroes will be readily recognizable until the American public, like the Constitution, becomes color-blind.

When Gunnar Myrdal completed his classic study, *The American Dilemma,* in the early 1940s, he was deeply pessimistic about the outlook for Negroes, particularly in the economic realm. They were, he found, at the very bottom of the occupational ladder, with little hope of rising in light of their limited education and skills, the large number of better-educated and more highly skilled whites then still unemployed, and the powerful, ever present discrimination to which they were exposed. Since Myrdal wrote, however, important changes have taken place in the status of the Negro with the removal of some, though not all, of the barriers to his full participation in American society.

The daily newspapers carry so many reports of exacerbated race relations, not only in the deep South but also in the border states and in the North, that it is sometimes difficult to gain perspective about what is now happening to the Negro throughout the country. It is even more difficult to estimate what is likely to happen in the future, due to the claims and counter-claims of those who favor change and those who defend the status quo. The confusion is vastly compounded by the fact that many of the assumptions once true about race relations in the United States, for example, that the Negro would be moderate in his demands for equality and passive in his approach, as well as the assumption by the Southern white leadership that it alone would decide what changes would take place, and how soon, are no longer valid, and it will probably not be long before they are completely irrelevant.

Since we have dealt with the major outlines of the Negro's economic improvement since Myrdal's book in our own study, *The Negro Potential*, we will call attention in the present context only to those developments that bear specifically on the changing values and goals of young people, particularly young Negroes.

For more generations than one likes to remember, Negroes growing up in the South, even the urban South, could look forward only to a dead end as laborers. At best, if they managed to graduate from college, they might get teaching jobs in segregated schools. The situation in the North was only slightly better. There were, of course, a limited number of opportunities, North and South, for Negroes to earn substantial incomes by catering to fellow Negroes—such as in insurance, funeral parlors, retailing, banking, and construction. But in general the outlook was bleak, particularly because the South had a surplus of white workers who, according to the mores of segregation, had the right to pre-empt whatever limited occupational opportunities there were.

Most young Negroes in past generations grew up in a bifurcated world, one in which the national ideology preached that the ambitious, self-reliant person could rise as high as his ability would take him, while in fact, the Negro, whatever his ambition, could look forward to little more than menial labor. And this low ceiling on Negro jobs reenforced attitudes and traditions stemming from the earlier slave society, when working hard and planning for the future made little sense. Since the Negro could never look forward to enjoying the fruits of his labor under slavery, much of his ingenuity was devoted to avoiding strenuous work. Plantation owners wanted field hands and nothing more, so at the time of their emancipation, Negroes were capable of being little else.

In perspective we can see that emancipation was mainly a negative act. The Negro was no longer the chattel of his owner. But neither the North nor the South cared to give him the support he needed to become truly free. Though slowly afforded an opportunity to become literate, the Negro received little else by way of help. In fact, it was not long before the organs of state and local government began to confine and restrict him, enacting laws specifically designed to insure that he never be permitted to enjoy the rights of freedom formally granted him.

Thorough segregation was a device to keep the Negro in a permanent second-class status, one which permitted him to have access only to inferior education, to unskilled jobs, and to social services far below the level available to the white population. Above all, segregation aimed to crush the Negro's hopes and aspirations.

As suggested earlier, 1940 can be considered the watershed for the Negro's accelerated progress. The extensive restrictions of the pre-World War II period have given way to considerably enlarged opportunities that presage even greater opportunities in the years ahead. But it is not easy for the Negro youngster to know how to proceed, caught as he is between a powerful tradition of resignation and the new promise of opportunities.

As so frequently happens in times of rapid change, these young people receive less help than they should from their parents, teachers, and others. And much of guidance they receive is faulty, for the older generation tends to think in terms of its own experience, with little understanding of what is likely to happen to their children now that segregation is being attacked from so many quarters, including that of the youngsters themselves.

It is not easy, even for intelligent people, to understand how radically different the future can be from the past. Many have lost their fortunes, their freedom, or their very lives because they lacked the imagination to adapt themselves to the threat of inflation, a growing dictatorship, or the imminent outbreak of war. Small wonder, then, that many Negroes are unable to adjust their sights to the opportunities now open to them and the still greater ones that loom on the horizon.

One of the great advantages which immigrants of earlier days had on their arrival in the United States was the living testimony all around them of the progress that others like themselves had made by dint of hard work, savings, and planning for the future. While the Negro youngster growing up today has Marion Anderson, Ralph Bunche, Jackie Robinson, Judge William Hastie, and others of his race to serve as models, these exceptional accomplishments may not be as helpful a guide to the average Negro youngster as the knowledge that individuals not too different from himself have risen one or two rungs on the ladder. In many parts of the country, particularly in the North and West, the Negro population has made sufficient economic gains in recent years to provide a fit example for the younger generation, especially to the children of individuals who themselves have done well. But elsewhere young people are growing up where the disabilities of the past loom more

prominent than the promises of the future. And these people continue to account for a high proportion of young
Negroes.

As long as they expect little of the world and little of
themselves, they may be frustrated but not disappointed,
for having ventured little, they can lose little. If they respond, however, to the changes which are under way and
do their utmost to acquire an education and a skill, they will
still be discriminated against for reasons of their race. Such
discrimination will surely rob them of some, and perhaps
even a large part, of their just rewards.

Many young Negroes, harkening to tradition, adopt the
first approach. They give up without trying. The barriers,
they feel, are too great to overcome. But, with the underlying improvement in educational and economic opportunities has come a change in the outlook of other young
Negroes. They are now creating their own opportunities
and their actions have lent encouragement to the entire
Negro community. The record of the last few years is
clear: It is the young Negroes of the South who are in the
vanguard of the struggle for equality. It is they who are
the new leaders of their people. Here is a new challenge for
Negro youth, and a surprising number of them have risen
to it.

It may well be that the time has passed when young Negroes will question whether it is worth making the effort
to shape their own future. Now that their final emancipation is within sight, their attitudes and behavior should be
more purposeful and disciplined. Paradoxically, Negro
youths in the South, who face the greater hurdles, are providing most of the new leadership, for in the South the
issues are more sharply drawn. In some ways the greater

freedom that exists in the North makes the issues more confusing. Negro youths living in the North cannot focus their attentions on a single clear objective, such as eliminating all facets of legal segregation, which gives added meaning and direction to the struggle of Southern Negroes.

Among Negro leaders, there was some concern during the planning phase that the 1960 Golden Anniversary White House Conference on Children and Youth would not face up squarely to the issue of race relations. But their fears proved unwarranted, especially as far as youth delegates themselves were concerned. They catapulted the issue into a position of priority, discussed it with maturity, and adopted a strong resolution in favor of the speedy elimination of all aspects of racial discrimination. Although a minority from the Southern and border states pleaded for a more moderate resolution, the vast majority of delegates insisted on a strong recommendation calling for the speedy elimination of all forms of segregation from the fabric of our national life. Quite apparent in the heated discussion from the floor were the sincerity and eloquence of white and Negro speakers alike, who urged a speedy elimination of this national blemish.

Observers of student life have been impressed that the first issue to catch the imagination of college students since the 1930s has been the renewed struggle for civil rights. This holds for many white as well as Negro campuses, North as well as South. Admittedly, only a minority have been involved so far, but it is always a minority that responds to challenge.

There are two further aspects of the problem of race relations that have a distinct bearing on the aspirations of young people and that warrant at least brief attention. The first relates to the values and goals of successful Negroes and the implications these have for their children's development. Many successful Negroes have sought to provide their children with all of the opportunities that insure success in a white, middle-class society. Toward this end, many Southern leaders have sent their children North to prominent preparatory schools and to the socially as well as academically renowned colleges. Northern Negroes in a position to do so have also sought to send their children to these preferred schools and colleges.

At first it might seem that, in this respect, the successful Negro is acting like the successful immigrant of an earlier day, who likewise sought to close the gap between himself and the dominant groups in society as quickly as possible. But there may well be a significant difference in the strivings of the Negro today. The difference is not in what the Negro hopes to accomplish but rather in his attitudes towards the group from whence he comes. For most immigrants, success in this country did not lead to breaking the ties with less successful brethren whom they had left behind. The rich Irishman surely did not lose interest in Ireland's struggle for freedom, the rich Italian did not become indifferent to what was happening in his homeland, and the rich Jew did not ignore the plight of his coreligionists. While not all successful Negroes have turned their backs on the Southland, the truth is that too many of them have seen their salvation in terms of their personal achievement and this, in turn, has meant inadequate support for their still seriously handicapped brethren. Such disassociation has had deleterious effects on the welfare of the Negro community but none more serious than the loss of sorely-needed leadership. But this, too, has begun to change, now that Negroes, both in the North and in the South, are becoming an important political force, with increasing power to set forth their demands and to have them met. Many of the best opportunities for occupational advancement and social prestige for Negroes will come through politics and its rewards —positions as judges, superintendents of schools, welfare commissioners, even cabinet officers. Negro youths increasingly appreciate that their own future is indissolubly linked with the struggle to improve the well-being of their entire race.

While some white youths in the North, and a very few even in the South, have shown their sympathy and support for the Negro sit-in demonstrations, the vast majority of white youths are indifferent or even hostile. In view of their parents' attitudes, their own lack of concern about the problem of civil rights is not surprising. Too little attention has been paid to the attitudes of Northern white adults when they come face to face with the integration of a school or the admission of Negro tenants to a residential area. All too frequently those who have been vociferous in their criticism of Southern segregationists see only the obstacles when it comes to improving the opportunities for Negroes in their own community. They do not object, in principle, to broadening Negro opportunities, but they do feel that they should not be asked to pay the price, jeopardizing educational standards or realty values. It may be a very human response to consider one's own self-interest first, last, and always, but its impact on the young should not be minimized. Young people early recognize when their parents are less than certain about the basic equality of white and Negro. Although they may grow up without any deep-seated antagonisms towards the Negro, they nonetheless are not free from varying orders of prejudice, dislike, uneasiness, or simply lack of concern. And as long as the indoctrination of the young remains as confused as it is on this most important aspect of our national life, much valuable energy of young and old, black and white alike will continue to be dissipated. Nor does the point lose its poignancy simply because it has been made before. Unless the United States can develop a mature and reasonable attitude towards the Negro, it will not be able to convince the Asians and Africans that it is the defender of human freedom and democracy. And if the United States fails on this effort, all men, whatever the color of their skin, may lose their freedom.

* IX

GUIDANCE

The preceding chapters should have firmly established the importance of guidance for the improvement of youth. After their tracing of the impact of the new psychology, the repercussions of the recent transformation in the nature of work, the crucial role of the school in molding the child, the complexities and implications of occupational, military, and marital choice, and the special problems which women and Negroes face, the tasks of guidance should be obvious. In fact, it is hard to conceive how a child could reach maturity without it. The question is not whether there should be guidance but who should give it, how much effort should go into it, and how can it be improved.

Guidance has an old and distinguished history, having been practiced by many different people through the ages. Those whose influence is often greatest, however, sometimes fail to appreciate the weight their words carry. Few physicians, teachers, ministers, or even friends realize how great an impact their casual suggestions can have on insecure parents hoping to give their child some direction in life. And the forces at work in modern America are such as to make parents less and less secure about their own abilities to guide their children—the continuing growth of knowledge, the rapid transformation of institutions, the lessening respect accorded tradition, the growing emphasis on not damaging the child's psyche. As a result of these forces, the importance of guidance is coming to be more and more appreciated.

THE GOALS OF GUIDANCE

The difficulties of defining the boundaries of guidance are many. There are some who would argue against defining any boundary. To do so, they would argue, is artificial. Since human beings, at every stage of life, are confronted with problems which their own knowledge and experience are insufficient to resolve, they are continuously forced to call on experts, or at least on those with greater knowledge and experience. And to the extent that parents do discuss their problems with their spouses, their friends, and even on occasion with professionally trained counselors, this contention has merit. However, in focusing on broadened opportunities for youth, we can identify four major areas of guidance. In each of these areas, parents and children are likely to face problems with which their own knowledge and experience ill equip them to cope.

There are, first of all, the problems connected with education. Which school should a child attend, which curriculum should he pursue, and at which point is the further investment of time, effort, and money no longer justified? Even the well-educated professional man, no less than the semi-skilled laborer, is quite unlikely to have the knowledge and background to exercise sound judgment in these areas. And the more the educational scene changes, the more difficult it becomes to exercise sound judgment. Here, clearly, is a major area of guidance.

Closely related to, though still distinguished from, the foregoing are the problems connected with occupational choice. This is a process, as we have seen, that goes on largely while the young person is still in school. On the one hand, he has to commit himself sufficiently to a certain occupational goal so that he can learn enough about the field to decide whether he really would like to pursue it and whether he has the ability to succeed in it. On the other hand, he does not want to commit himself any more than need be, for otherwise he will unnecessarily close out alternative channels of development. Once again the factors discussed in previous chapters make it difficult for young people to avoid either premature commitment or wasteful indecision. Here, too, is a major area for guidance.

Less clearly recognized but also important are the problems connected with military service and marriage. High schools and colleges, for the most part, have failed to recognize their responsibility for providing information about military service. Yet this is another area in which the young person himself and his parents as well have little knowledge or experience. How many college men realize, for example, how important it may be to have been in the armed services if they hope one day to enter active politics? It is important not only for their record but also for the opportunity it will give them to meet Americans from varying regions and backgrounds.

In the area of marital decision, guidance is probably less feasible and has probably less chance of success. Still, guidance in this area may make a rational decision more likely. The importance of completing college or professional education, the income level necessary to maintain a certain accustomed standard of living, the possibility of a wife working while her children are still young, the depth of religious, ethnic, and racial attitudes—all these are important considerations in rational mate selection. Once a young person is in love, it may be difficult to impress him with the importance of these considerations; but at an earlier age, when he is still in the process of exploration, making him aware of these factors may well be possible. Besides, the fact that guidance may prove difficult is no reason not to try it.

Finally, there are the problems connected with those young people who deviate from the norm—those who are above average in intelligence and maturity and those who are below average. The parents of these children have a special need for guidance so that they can better understand their offspring's needs and act to meet them.

The need for guidance is especially pressing for those parents whose children are growing up in an environment undergoing radical transformation. Such is the case in many farm communities, depressed industrial areas, and desegregated Negro neighborhoods. Another type of radical change is affecting the life-work patterns of women, who for the first time in history can concentrate their child-rearing activities into a relatively few years and devote the remaining decades to meaningful occupational activity. As young women approach adulthood, they need to be made aware of these expanding opportunities.

THE TWO FACES OF GUIDANCE

Perhaps this is the place to point out that the concept of guidance we have been using has two facets. The first focuses on those responsible for rearing and training the young, particularly parents and teachers. During the earliest years of his life, the child is totally dependent on others. His role is passive and he acquires his emotional and intellectual coloring from those around him. Direct guidance of the child at this stage of his life is usually not possible. The only way guidance can be effective is by influencing the adults who will control the child's development. Efforts to help youth must be aimed at them.

In puberty and more particularly in adolescence the focus shifts, as the youngster begins to assume increasing responsibility for his own direction. It is he who must decide what he wants to be when he grows up, and it is he who must put forth the necessary effort, first in school and later at work. At this point, the youth himself becomes the object of guidance.

As an adolescent, a young person is primarily concerned with learning more about himself—what kind of person he is and more important what kind of person he can become. Here, guidance can be particularly useful, showing him how he can move from where he is to where he would like to be. It can enable him to assess his own capabilities and it can show him how to exploit these capabilities. It can prevent him from making an unwise, premature commitment, and it can tell him how much experience he needs before he will be able to properly evaluate a particular career goal.

As a young adult, the individual usually has developed a sense of identity. Now he is concerned with learning about the conditions that prevail in the world into which he must fit himself. And there is so much he needs to know about the world of work, the military, and family and social relationships. The function of guidance has shifted, but it still remains important.

Although the areas for guidance are considerable, they are not unlimited. The effectiveness of guidance will de-

pend to a large extent on the capacity of parents to understand the advice they have been given and to act upon it.
The insights of the new psychology, for example, can be
utilized only by parents who have some degree of education
and who are not too severely handicapped by old beliefs
and practices. In many instances, regrettably, such pre-
requisites do not exist. Even more limiting are such factors
as type of work, income, location, and community preju-
dices, aspects of which do so much to shape and control
the lives of adults and therefore determine what they can
do for their children. Of these factors, family income may
well be the most important, for family income determines
to such a great extent the environment in which a child is
brought up.

As young people approach the time when they must make
important decisions about their future work and life, they
find themselves being forced to make certain educational
choices. At a certain date they must choose a school, a
program, and a major. But at the same time, teachers and
counselors are standing by, ready to help them make a
choice. Were it not for this readily available guidance,
many young people would flounder, even more than they
now do.

But when these young people reach adulthood, institutional pressures no longer force them to face up squarely
to certain alternatives. Opportunities for guidance may
still exist but whether or not they will be used depends
to a much larger extent on the individual. Unless he takes
the first step to seek guidance, nothing will happen. And
regrettably, many people who are most in need of help are
unacquainted with the ways of securing it or are blocked
emotionally from seeking it.

WHAT GUIDANCE CAN DO

Since each reader has probably defined guidance in terms of his own knowledge and experience, it might be well to set out briefly what appear to be the five main ways in which guidance can contribute to the fuller development of young people.

For one thing, guidance can provide general information to the parents of young children or to young people directly. It can inform them of the opportunities open to them, the barriers they must overcome, and the types of special assistance available—essential information if a young person is to develop his potential in full.

A second and very important function that guidance can perform is "intervention." The individual in a quandary, who needs help, can frequently gain new insight into his problem with the aid of a counselor. Instead of being concerned with a symptom—the original precipitant of his seeking assistance—the individual may, under the promptings of a specialist, come to recognize for the first time that the heart of his problem lies elsewhere, in an area that he had not earlier perceived, no less investigated.

Another way that guidance can help young people is through various forms of objective assistance. The counselor can tell a young person where to apply for college admission, how to fill out a fellowship application, or where to look for summer employment. In these days, with the pressure for admission to college becoming more intense, with scholarship funds growing rapidly, with distances being sharply reduced—with the environment undergoing so many and such radical changes, the need for objective information has never been greater.

As a young person matures, he inevitably experiences some crisis when he becomes shaken, confused, or depressed. Sometimes the cause is the sudden loss of a beloved one; at other times it may reflect a grievous disappointment; at still others it may be a combination of factors. In any case, however, guidance can help the young person over a difficult hump. Such support may be limited to only one or a few consultations, or it may stretch over a longer period. In the absence of gross pathology, however, the young tend to grow out of their troubles, especially if they can get a helping hand when they need it. As our study, *The Ineffective Soldier,* made clear, even young men seriously disturbed by their combat experiences were, in many cases, able to make a rapid recovery with only a little help.

Between general support and psychotherapy, there is a narrow no man's land. One of the most useful services that a counselor can perform is to recognize this boundary line, to spot that minority of young people whose problems are so deeply rooted in emotional conflict that they require help from psychotherapists. Once again, the type and intensity of the help may vary greatly, from relatively few sessions to a much longer period of treatment.

Guidance thus covers a wide range: information, intervention, objective assistance, support and clarification, and psychotherapy—but therein lies much of its strength. Children and young people as they grow up need help at various stages of their lives to gain greater insight into themselves, into others with whom they are in close contact, and into the world of reality.

SPECIAL CHILDREN: THE PROBLEM OF DELINQUENCY

So far, we have discussed the average child only. While he may at some point in his life experience an emotional crisis, by and large he is not seriously disturbed. There are others, however, considerable in number, who deviate quite significantly from the norm and thus present a special challenge to guidance. And the more they deviate from the norm, the more difficulty they will have in making a satisfactory adjustment in the family, the school, and the community. Since parents and teachers are more accustomed to dealing with the typical child, they are usually unable to cope with the atypical. Moreover, the basic institutions of society, those most intimately concerned with children, are also geared to meet the needs of the average, not the deviant, child.

The stages through which a child deviates from the norm can best be illustrated by setting out schematically what might for lack of a better term be called the social history of the delinquent. The emphasis here is on the term social, to underscore the fact that the difficulty often lies in the inadequacy of conventional institutions, particularly the school, in meeting the needs of deviant children.

When a child enters elementary school, society makes its first demand on him. He must adapt himself to an institution in which he will spend the greater part of each week for at least ten years. For any one of three reasons, however, he may fail to make the necessary adjustment. For one thing, he may lack the intellectual capability to keep abreast of his classmates, and he may fall behind in learning how to read, spell, and do arithmetic. In fact, if he is seriously retarded, he may fail to make any progress whatsoever.

But it is equally probable that his difficulties may lie elsewhere. He may have superior intelligence and still be unable to learn, if he is in such emotional turmoil, in such personality conflict that most of his energies are drained. In that case, he may not be able to make even that minimum of effort required to absorb new knowledge.

There is also a third possibility. A child does not necessarily have to have a serious emotional problem to fail to adjust to school. He may simply be in great conflict, for a variety of reasons, with one or both of his parents. The antagonism toward his parents may then be transferred to his teachers, with the result that he cannot absorb what his teachers are trying to instill in him.

There is no need here to go back of the disturbance of the learning process, to trace the variety of social, familial, and individual factors that may be responsible for the child's difficulty in learning. Rather we are concerned with what happens once the disturbance occurs.

As the child begins to fall behind, his school experience becomes increasingly unpleasant. Not only does he become acutely aware of his own deficiencies, he is also cut off from social contacts with other children his own age since, while he remains behind, they move on to higher grades. His failure in school, moreover, inevitably leads to tension at home, even in those homes where parents place little value on education. The parents will resent being called to school to hear complaints that their child is lagging behind the others, and they will communicate this resentment to the child, even if unintentionally. This will further strain the relationships within the home, contributing to the pressures which made learning so difficult for the child in the first place.

In short, the child who fails to fit into the school's mold is headed for a rough time. His failure in the classroom will deprive him of the friendship of children his own age, most of whom will soon pass him by on the educational ladder.

It will also exacerbate the relations with his own family, since they will scorn him for his failure and rebuke him for the trouble which that failure causes them.

Rejected by other children his own age as well as by his own family, it is not surprising that the castoffs and the failures, the emotionally disturbed and the hostile, should gravitate towards each other. They, too, have a need to belong, if only to a group whose members have no more in common than the fact that they are in conflict with their parents and teachers.

As these conflicts intensify—as they surely will with increasing frustration in school—these youngsters will begin resorting to aggressive behavior. In so "acting out" their own personality problems, they are prone to come into conflict with law enforcement authorities, who must repress or punish their aberrant behavior. This in turn only leads to more serious delinquency and more drastic punishment. The failure of most communities to provide an effective alternative for the child who fails to adjust to school makes this type of antisocial behavior take on more serious proportions. As the educational system is presently structured, minor problems inevitably grow into major ones.

The later history of most delinquents lends substance to this interpretation of the dynamics of antisocial behavior. For once many of these youngsters are freed from the necessity of continuing in school, once they get a job, earn money and associate with adults, their frustration often disappears and in turn, their delinquent behavior frequently ceases.

Unfortunately, in an increasingly technical society, the failure of many young people to acquire adequate education is making this transition to adulthood more difficult, for without adequate education, the chances of obtaining and holding on to a satisfying job are greatly reduced. Of all the things that society can do to reduce the pathology out of which delinquency is spawned, none promises greater success than a fundamental change in the educational system so that even children with serious handicaps can acquire basic skills and enjoy satisfying socializing experiences.

ADJUSTMENT POTENTIAL

From our three volume study, *The Ineffective Soldier,* there emerged the important theoretical concept of "adjustment potential." Our detailed investigation of the complex factors that determine performance levels in civilian and military life led us to conclude that it was an error to single out any one characteristic—such as emotional stability—to explain what makes people succeed or fail in their life tasks. What is needed is a broad concept which includes the whole gamut of a man's strengths and weaknesses. Such a concept should also include the effect of organizational structure and social environment interacting with the individual's personality.

The concept of adjustment potential has clear relevance to understanding and strengthening guidance. It suggests that the development of young people must be considered in a broad framework, one which includes the strengths and weaknesses of the family, the school, and the community, as well as the strengths and weaknesses of the young people themselves. What guidance can or cannot do, the conditions under which it can or cannot succeed—these basic conditions become more clearly recognizable once the concept of adjustment potential is introduced.

THE LIMITS OF GUIDANCE

The focus of our discussion has been primarily on the individual—what can be done to enable him to make better use of his capabilities and opportunities. But this emphasis on the individual and what he himself can achieve should not obscure the extent to which large social forces determine the type of work a person will do when he grows up and the type of life he will lead. For example, the expansion of educational facilities will play a larger role in determining the number of engineers in the 1970s than the admonitions of admirals and generals that the Soviet Union is overtaking the United States in science. Similarly, the future of those young Americans growing up on farms will be determined by the rate at which the technological revolution in agriculture continues and, more particularly, the rate at which the industrial and service sectors of the economy expand. In like manner, the future of Negro children will be determined by the rate at which opportunities once closed to them in education, social relations, and employment are opened up.

The great importance of social forces should not lead anyone to conclude that guidance does not count, that the other factors are too powerful to be overcome. The recognition of these powerful social forces should however lead to an awareness of how complex an undertaking guidance is, of how its effectiveness is determined by the interplay of uncontrollable institutional factors outside the individual's control and his own will.

What we have tried to show is the importance of guidance, so that young people can get the help they often need.

Furthermore, guidance is never the task of any one person —whether it be parent, teacher, or counselor—but is the task of all those who come into contact with young people. If no one person alone can assume the responsibility for guiding the young, so too, no one who comes in contact with them can avoid the duty, the challenge, and the opportunity of giving guidance to those who need it. Regrettably, many adults, fearful of the responsibility, seek refuge behind the doctrine that the young should make their own decisions.

* X

REALISTIC ASSUMPTIONS

Americans, as we have seen, have a deep, and apparently continuing, optimism about their capacity to change the environment for the better. Moreover, a change in the environment, it is felt, will lead to an improvement of youth by providing the younger generation with greater opportunities than were available to the old. This basic optimism is reflected in the doctrine of perfectability, a doctrine which has had several important consequences.

It created a most favorable background for accepting the new as well as for discarding the old. While this positive stance toward change was in general a beneficial one, it was not without its drawbacks, some of them quite serious. The perfectability doctrine, as we have seen, frequently led reformers to overlook the objective circumstances, genetic and social, that sometimes make accomplishing a desirable objective impossible. The deep hold of the perfectability doctrine, while it provided invaluable motive power for the protagonists of change, also had the disadvantage—and sometimes it was a serious one—of blocking sound and sensible appraisals of what might, in fact, be accomplished. Serious barriers which simply could not be wished away often remained unrecognized or, worse, were ignored. The inevitable result, in many cases, was disappointment, disillusionment, and a serious waste of resources. The preceding chapters have revealed an underlying dualism between the belief in human perfectability and the realities of contemporary American life. This dualism should be explored in greater depth in the five areas most directly related to the improvement of youth: the individual, the family, the school, government, and knowledge. Such a confrontation of assumptions and realities should help to delineate more sharply than was possible in the earlier chapters the potentialities and limitations of society's efforts to improve its youth.

THE INDIVIDUAL

Underlying the perfectability doctrine is the fundamental assumption that all individuals, by nature and surely by cultural exposure, want to improve themselves and will do so if given the opportunity. The settlement and development of this country can only be understood in these terms —that millions from abroad, and millions of native born were willing and able to put forth the sustained effort required to tame the rugged environment and to push the agricultural and later the industrial economy from the Atlantic seaboard to the Pacific. They were willing to put forth this great effort because they saw that their own salvation, or at least their opportunity for vast improvement, was intimately linked to this undertaking. American history, therefore, supports the belief that men are not only willing but eager to improve themselves.

But the optimists failed to perceive some important limitations. There were, first, the many Americans who, like people in every society, because of limited intellectual endowment were simply not able to take more than limited advantage of the opportunities available to them. While they were able to improve themselves somewhat, the fact remains that limitations arising at birth have limited the accomplishments of a significant segment of the total population. Hence the ability of society to affect their development by improvement and manipulation of the environment is highly restricted.

Society is similarly limited in what it can do for children with severe emotional disorders. Once again the early years of life may bring so many emotional scars that a large number of young people, including some relatively well endowed intellectually, will never be able to take advantage of the opportunities open to them. Here, too, the expansion of facilities geared especially to their needs can do much to improve their situation. But the sad fact remains that there are many families in the United States who, despite adequate financial resources, have been unable to transform a seriously disturbed child into a well-functioning adult. It is necessary to recognize that because of their emotional instability many young people will be unable to take anything like full advantage of their environmental opportunities. Nor is there any reason to expect that if society substantially increased these opportunities the outcome would be much different. Unfortunately, a person's defects themselves usually make it impossible for him to avail himself of opportunities, whether limited or expanded.

While intellectual shortcomings and emotional instability represent the major qualifications of the doctrine that each individual wants to improve himself, there is a third limitation. Lack of motivation, an outgrowth frequently of intellectual limitations or emotional instability, may sometimes be independent of them and requires recognition as an additional factor.

The belief that a universal desire for self improvement

characterized earlier generations is probably a misreading of American history. Scholars, impressed by the large numbers who were enterprising and energetic, simply postulated that this attribute was characteristic of all Americans. But whatever the truth may be for generations past, it cannot be seriously questioned that a sizable proportion of today's young people are not motivated—for whatever complex reasons—to do their best. Lacking such motivation, they cannot take advantage of the opportunities our society has to offer them. And if the available opportunities were increased, there is no reason to believe they would respond very differently.

In brief, the assumption that every individual will try to do his best does not always hold true. There are, and there probably always will be, a large number of young people who, lacking the necessary intellectual capacity, emotional stability, or strong motivation, will be unable to take full advantage of the opportunities available to them. It follows from this that a marked expansion of those opportunities would not seriously alter the outcome.

While some of the children unable to make the most of their opportunities come from middle or even upper income families, there are many others whose intellectual retardation, emotional instability, or lack of motivation reflects to a large degree the poverty and lack of stimulation in their homes. As the old saying puts it, the most important thing a child can do is to pick the right parents. Regrettably, a great many children are unlucky. They may be born into a disadvantaged minority group; their parents may not be living together; the money coming into the household may be inadequate; or all of these things may be true. To make matters worse, such disadvantaged families tend to live in close proximity. A depressing atmosphere then tends to permeate the neighborhood and the institutions located therein—the school, the church, and the recreational facilities.

Such oppressive family and social environments interfere seriously with the intellectual, emotional, and motivational development of young people exposed to them. They may so cripple and atrophy young people's potential in early childhood that they are unable at a later stage of their development—after they start school—to avail themselves of the opportunities which could enable them to overcome their initial handicaps. While it is true that some youngsters can, in ways that we do not really comprehend, surmount the oppressive circumstances under which they have grown up, most young people, understandably enough, cannot do so. They carry the scars with them throughout the whole of their lives.

The belief is widely held that what happens to an individual depends entirely on him. While it is well to place great responsibility on the individual for his own development and welfare, it simply is not true that the serious failure of so many deprived children is due to their own personal shortcomings and deficiencies. Life is hard, and many children never get even the minimum break needed to achieve eventual success in life. An indiscriminate doctrine of personal responsibility can be very discouraging. It can weaken still further what little motivation deprived youngsters may have acquired to better themselves, by creating not only frustration but a deep sense of guilt.

THE FAMILY

Society wisely places the primary responsibility on parents for the care and nurturing of their offspring. While the crucial role of parents has long been appreciated, recent advances in dynamic psychology have emphasized some of the more subtle and pervasive influences arising out of even the earliest relationships between young children and their parents. Admittedly, parents have very wide scope to influence, for better or worse, what happens to their offspring. But this influence is limited.

While death has caused family disruption far less frequently in recent decades than in the past, it cannot be ignored even today. Many children still lose their fathers or mothers, and the impact of such a loss is likely to be profound, even under otherwise favorable circumstances. If family disruption through the premature death of a parent has become less frequent, family disruption from divorce has greatly increased. Thus many young people still grow up with one rather than two parents.

Moreover, the severe illness of a parent, especially the mother of very young children, can prove almost as unsettling as death. Such severe illness, while on the decrease, is still relatively widespread. There is also a much larger group of parents who, though alive and healthy, are for a variety of reasons unable to earn enough to provide adequately for their offspring. Hence, while the family has the primary responsibility for the proper nurturing of the young, many families, for reasons beyond their control, are unable to discharge this responsibility.

In addition to those afflicted by major misfortune or serious social pathology, there are a great many more families which face serious barriers in seeking to fulfill their task of child rearing. Severe limitations of intellectual capacity or educational background make it very difficult, and frequently impossible, for many parents to take advantage of much that is new and constructive. They are simply unable to avail themselves of important new knowledge bearing on the physical, emotional, or educational development of their offspring. The numbers so handicapped run into the millions.

In many families, parents are forced to invest the greater part of their energies in caring for a seriously defective child. As a result, they are unable to do as much as they would like to for their other children. These other children may be neglected, and if this neglect is substantial, permanent damage may ensue. Once again, ill fortune creates conditions that even able people cannot readily surmount entirely on their own.

So far we have discussed only the pathological situations likely to interfere with the ability of parents to nurture their children adequately. But there remains one condition, generic to family life, which is always present and which is always disturbing, and sometimes even destructive. No family, no matter how well-endowed with intelligence, income, and social status, can escape intramural conflict and crisis. It is inherent in the cycle of growth itself. In the development of the young there are certain times when these struggles are heightened—at three or four when the child must loosen its hold on its mother; and again at puberty when it must come to grips with the emergence of its sexuality. These struggles between parents and children can not be worked out without some residue of permanent frustration, hostility, and aggression. This means that the young, no matter how understanding and sympathetic their parents may be, will nonetheless grow up with some emotional scarring. While parents can, with understanding and forbearance, keep the scarring within tolerable limits, they cannot prevent it entirely. When one adds to this the further fact that children have varying thresholds for tolerating such conflict, one realizes that, important as parents are in the nurturing of the young, there is much over which they have little or no control. Theirs is a limited, not an unlimited, liability.

THE SCHOOL

School represents, next to the family, the most important institution in the training of young people. It is not surprising that, having recognized the crucial role that schools play in the development of the young and having invested large sums in their support, the American public continues to look to the school to shape the next generation along the lines which it desires. While the school can go far toward meeting this truly overwhelming responsibility, severe limitations preclude its ever fulfilling the more exaggerated claims made on it.

The nation's educational plant is a complex undertaking representing the largest single unit in the economy. Deeply embedded in the governmental structure, the school system is particularly exposed to public opinion. For these and still other reasons it cannot be easily modified or changed. Control is splintered among literally thousands of school boards, the membership of which is in turn divided over objectives and methods. Hence it is difficult to correct what has been found faulty in the schools just as it is difficult to introduce what is new or promising. This inherent difficulty of bringing about change inevitably tends to frustrate those who are imaginative and enterprising, driving them from the school systems in despair. As a result, the schools are left with those teachers and administrators who can more readily make their peace with things as they are.

The rigidity of its structure is not the only thing that pre-
vents the school from more successfully fulfilling its responsibility. There is the important matter of resources—
buildings, operating funds, and staff. While more money
would help, the problem cuts deeper. With the school system requiring about two million teachers—about eight
times as many teachers as there are physicians in the country
—it is virtually impossible to place a well qualified teacher
in every classroom.

Funds and staffing aside, the school faces still further difficulties. What it can accomplish is limited by what the
community wants it to accomplish. As Dr. James Conant has
made clear in several of his recent reports, the superintendents in many schools are judged mainly by their ability
to develop a winning football team. While schools that
spend more money per pupil generally do a better job of
educating their young people, there are many suburban
communities where, despite relatively high per capita expenditures on education, the academic achievement is relatively low. The reason for this is not hard to see. While the
school can do something and the exceptional school can
do much to overcome a lack of interest in intellectual
achievement in the home, what the school can actually accomplish along these lines is nonetheless limited.

Most teachers, it is probably safe to assume, would point
to lack of motivation as the major barrier to their pupils'
learning. And there is little prospect, despite the recent
growing emphasis on the importance of a good education
for later success in life, that this barrier will soon be removed.

The large number of handicapped children is another
serious obstacle that the school faces. The essential services

which these children need if they are to receive any education at all, such as testing and guidance clinics, teachers
skilled in remedial reading, psychiatric consultants, and
sometimes even special schools, often do not exist or exist
to such a limited extent that they cannot help more than a
small percentage of those in need. As a result, many teachers must devote a good part of their time and energy simply
to keeping these handicapped children under control while
at the same time they try to instruct those capable of making
normal progress. The result more often than not is that
neither the handicapped child nor the rest of the class receives needed attention.

As an example of the inherent rigidity noted earlier, the
school has been unable to develop any method of instruction other than classroom attendance for a stipulated number of hours per day. The fact is that in junior and senior
high school many students are capable of doing a considerable amount of work on their own, but the present system precludes this possibility. While some schools are an
exception, the overwhelming majority have not found it
practical to include provision for independent study within
the curriculum. Exposed as a result to long, boring hours in
the classroom, many young people lose their enthusiasm
for learning.

Finally, the school has not yet recognized the extent to
which it is no longer uniquely responsible for education.
Only a few years ago, the formal school was the sole focus
of the nation's educational effort. Today the armed services, industry, and a vast array of adult educational facilities
supplement the basic institutions. The school, however, has
not yet fully appreciated the growth of these ancillary educational efforts. It has not met its responsibility to see that

its graduates are motivated to make greater use of these vastly expanded opportunities.

If only the school succeeds in instilling in its pupils a respect for learning, and provides them with the basic skills they will need later in life, it will have done its job well. The extent to which it succeeds in this undertaking will depend in large measure on how well it alone does its job. But it will also depend on the external environment—on the type of home and community into which its pupils are born. While there is much that the school can do to improve youth, there are areas where its success depends on help from the outside.

GOVERNMENT

The government, federal, state, and local, can do a good deal to provide young people with a more suitable environment for developing their capabilities. Without question, the most important single thing the government does is to provide the necessary financial support for the school. In many parts of the United States public education now extends from kindergarten to graduate school. Substantial sums are made available for the support of the comprehensive system, even though they fall short, for the reasons previously noted as well as for the reasons to be outlined below, of the level which would assure all children equal opportunity.

But there is much else that government has been able to contribute to the more effective development of the young. For a significant minority of families, where there is no breadwinner or where he is unable to earn by his own efforts a wage sufficient to support all who are dependent on him, the government provides an income so that the family will remain intact and the children will have the bare essentials.

In recent decades, government has gone far beyond this basic relief by investing considerable sums in housing for low income families, in various types of medical services, and in recreational facilities, all of which play an important role in the development of the young.

But the reach of government is even greater. In recent years it has vastly expanded its efforts to provide special services for disadvantaged children. For instance, most progressive states have greatly increased their support of programs to aid mentally retarded and emotionally disturbed children, predelinquent and delinquent youngsters, children from culturally deprived homes, and many others whose parents are unable to provide for them adequately. Admittedly, few if any communities have done all that is needed to give every child a chance to start life without a handicap. But the serious shortcomings that remain should not obscure the major gains that have been made.

Powerful as government is, especially the federal government, there are good as well as bad reasons why it has not been able to meet all the needs of the young and why it may not be able to meet them in the future. The resources of government are not unlimited. In a democracy the people must agree to the taxes that are levied on them—at least their representatives must determine the rates at which they are to be taxed. Even if the people and their representatives should acknowledge the urgent needs of children, adequate sums may not be forthcoming because the same people and their representatives may also acknowledge the powerful claims of other groups—the aged, the sick, the unemployed. At the national level, the needs of children must compete against the demands of national security and the race into space with the Russians. While we could doubtless do much more than we are doing at present to meet the needs of young people, these other, often high priority, claims on government funds will continue to push aside the claims of children.

But the scramble for limited tax dollars is only part of the story. There is also the lack of qualified personnel. While raising salaries and reducing the cost of training will undoubtedly produce more qualified personnel, the fact remains that the combination of talent and aptitude required for such positions is sufficiently rare that government would be unable to attract the additional professionals required even if it were to expand its services to children.

To make matters worse, those state and local governments which have the greatest difficulty raising money are the very ones which have the greatest need for additional services to children. While part of this difficulty can be overcome by increased federal grants, these poorer localities still have the problem of securing sufficient numbers of trained personnel. There is no escaping the fact that under a federal system the national government is unlikely to do more than establish minimum services. Anything above this minimum will usually require the expenditure of state or private funds.

For with many programs competing for support, the best chance of the federal government's satisfying unmet needs is to provide a basic level of support. To do more for some would require it to ignore others.

But even if the potentialities of governmental action were greater than they presently appear to be, it would be necessary to recognize that the government while it can provide opportunities, cannot insure that they will be used. What happens to young people, it must be emphasized once again, depends to a very large measure on the way they have been brought up and on the values they have absorbed in the process.

SCIENCE

Underpinning the American faith in perfectability is the belief that much that was impossible in the past will become possible in the future through the acquisition and application of new knowledge. And during the present century there has been repeated evidence of science's ability to reduce or eliminate known ills. Nothing has contributed more to the well-being of the young than the striking reduction in infant and child mortality as a result of scientific advances in biology and bacteriology. As was made clear in the earlier chapters of this book, radical advances in psychology and psychiatry have also contributed to the improvement of youth.

Were it not for this conviction that new knowledge will be continuously forthcoming—if only adequate talent, money, and time are devoted to the search for it—the prevailing belief that each successive generation should be able to do better than the last in the rearing of its young would not be so strong.

Few would argue that the solution to any current, seemingly insolvable problem will not be found eventually if enough effort is devoted to finding it. The dynamics of science thus reenforce the underlying optimistic lilt of American culture, especially where children are concerned. But while most things may be possible in the long run, science's ability to contribute to the improvement of youth, in the short run, may be limited.

The first and perhaps most important limitation inherent

in science itself is the fact that significant new ideas take time to be gestated. Admittedly the process of discovery can be affected by the amount and more particularly by the quality of the resources devoted to it; but there comes a point—and it may come quite early—where there is no effective substitution for time and talent. Basically significant and useful ideas make their appearance only infrequently. And the fact that society has great need for new understanding and control, as in the dramatic case of cancer, is no guarantee whatever that it will be forthcoming in the near future.

Scientific advances in the field of human, particularly child, behavior face a second formidable hurdle. One factor that has played an important role in the advances of the physical sciences has been the possibility of using laboratory experimentation. Under controlled conditions, a vast array of alternative approaches could be explored, observed, tested, and duplicated. No such opportunity, however, exists in the case of the behavioral sciences. Human beings are not fit subjects for laboratory experiments; it runs counter to the ethics of the Western world to submit healthy people to processes or procedures that may permanently injure them.

The difficulty of performing experiments on human beings places the student of human behavior at a serious disadvantage. His only option is to find a substitute method of inquiry, one that can provide some, if not all, of the laboratory experiment's advantages. One possibility is a carefully controlled study in which the development of children and young adults is studied over a period of many years. But, by definition, this is a very slow method—one that takes decades to complete. Furthermore, it is extremely costly to keep track of any large number of people over time in a country characterized by high mobility. Finally, the fact that people are being studied inevitably colors and distorts the results. While this type of study can be modified in various ways to reduce the time and cost, it suffers from other handicaps which are sufficiently serious so that the longitudinal study at best can be a limited instrument for acquiring new knowledge.

Even when new and significant ideas are wrested from the unknown by talented investigators able to surmount in one fashion or another the serious methodological difficulties outlined above, the relevance of what they may have discovered or clarified is not always self-evident. In a society that is open and friendly to the new, that is really eager to grasp at an answer because it has for so long been without one, there is a real danger that a new theoretical advance will be extended beyond its proper limits. Society may be asked to support programs which, if critically examined, would be found unjustified and unsuitable for accomplishing the purposes intended.

But the most serious hurdle of all relates to making the leap from an advance in theory to a large-scale social application. It was a relatively easy matter, once bacteriologists discovered that contaminated water and milk led to infection, to bring about the necessary changes in the way water and milk are processed so as to eliminate the danger to the public's health. Consider in contrast the difficulties of applying the new insights into the nature of emotional disorders. Although the new dynamic psychology has proved its worth, the numbers of skillful practitioners are relatively few and the course of treatment is usually long and costly. No sure or simple way has been found as yet to utilize this new knowledge to help the large numbers in our population who could profit from it. In short, the problem of application, relatively easy in much of preventive medicine, has proved in psychotherapy to be exceedingly complex and intractable.

While there are ample grounds for a long-term optimism about the ability of science to contribute even more in the future than in the past to the improvement of youth, extreme expectations in the short run are unwarranted.

PERFECTABILITY AND SOCIETY

One can now draw up a balance sheet, weighing the strengths against the weaknesses of American society's efforts to improve its youth. On the asset side is the basically optimistic conviction of the society that youth can be improved. This is a powerful factor in bringing about needed change, for it establishes a favorable disposition to try something new and to discard the old. Next there is the willingness to risk sizable investments in new programs that appear promising. Also on the asset side is the society's underlying pragmatism, which enables it to try new ideas and new approaches without worrying about any unforeseen secondary effects. The complexity of things social is so great that in the absence of this healthy pragmatism no change would be ventured.

So much for the assets—and valuable assets they are. But optimism, even when backed by large-scale investment and tempered by a pragmatic outlook on social change, has its drawbacks. It has been a major objective of this book to broaden the reader's perspective into the inherent limitations of the perfectability doctrine when applied to youth. Attention was directed to factors, individual and social, that militate against the steady forward sweep of progress on all fronts. It was found that potent as money is, it cannot by itself insure the successful elimination of all barriers to improvement. Many were found to be deeply imbedded in heredity, in cultural tradition, in structure of family life, in lack of knowledge. Each may eventually be overcome, but not easily or quickly.

The accomplishment of a major purpose always involves the effective deployment of assets as well as the skilful avoidance of obstacles. Clarifying the perfectability doctrine's limitations, therefore, should strengthen the efforts aimed at improving youth.

* XI

DIRECTIONS FOR POLICY

Our purpose has been to analyze and interpret, not to formulate proposals and programs for action. It has been an effort at perspective, not at persuasion. But a book on the improvement of youth that avoids all policy recommendations would probably leave the reader with a dissatisfied feeling, for he could most properly ask what are the policy implications of the analysis. While conceptual contributions have a part to play in progress, action remains the payoff.

This concluding chapter cannot satisfy those who want to know what to do next, and what to do after that, to insure that young people in the United States have greater opportunities to develop and utilize their capabilities. Such a task far exceeds our objective. It may be worth noting that the 1960 White House Conference on Children and Youth formulated about seven hundred specific resolutions covering almost every aspect of the problems faced by children and young people in contemporary American society. These resolutions, together with a survey of the background materials and the discussions which contributed to their formulation, have been reproduced and are available to interested readers.

The aim of this chapter is much more modest. It will try to point out some of the policy implications of the foregoing analysis. Without listing a specific program, it will outline the important arenas where action is required. It will try, moreover, to make explicit the links between the earlier analysis and the areas for action which we are about to suggest.

Despite the qualifications we found it necessary to introduce, we are in full accord with the central teaching of the new psychology, which sees human development as a process in which early family experiences are of primary importance in shaping the child's personality. Hence, whenever families are characterized by serious disorders—economic, emotional, or other—the probability is very high indeed that some and often all of the children will grow up seriously damaged. It follows therefore that whatever instrumentalities a rich and humane society has at its disposal should be used to eliminate if possible, and compensate for if elimination is not possible, those conditions which are responsible for such severe disorders.

The courts have understandably been loath to forceably separate children from their parents, except in the face of strong evidence that the parents are totally unfit to care for their offspring. It may well be that this policy of reluctance to separate certain children from their parents needs reappraisal.

No society can ever compensate fully for the shortcomings of family life; yet it may well be that we are currently allowing children to remain with parents who cannot provide for them even minimally, simply because we have no suitable alternative. A judge, in deciding custody of a child, must make his decision in terms of existing realities, not hypothetical alternatives. If he has no place except already badly overcrowded public institutions where he can send abused or neglected children, he is probably wiser to leave them with their parents. But it does not follow that we cannot do much better than we have been doing to create such alternatives. The first challenge is to recognize the problem, and the second is to recognize that a failure to meet it will result in human misery and social waste.

But if substitute homes must be found for some children, improved homes are needed for many more. The United States in the 1930s established a system of public welfare which included, among other things, programs to strengthen the family and provide aid to dependent children. But the intervention of World War II and the succeeding years of prosperity deflected attention from these programs. Only recently have they come back into the spotlight, largely because of mounting criticism that, despite the expenditures of large sums of money, the programs are failing to accomplish their intended purposes. In fact, some of the most strident critics argue that the expenditures of these large sums, by encouraging personal irresponsibility, have worsened rather than improved the situation.

Much of this criticism is wide of the mark. It represents little more than the deep-seated hostility of certain groups to the expenditures of public funds for the support of the weak, the retarded, and the irresponsible, particularly when members of the Negro minority loom large among the recipients of such funds. But even those basically sympathetic to the disadvantaged and disturbed are coming to realize that an effective program requires more than the monthly disbursement of maintenance checks. Sorely handicapped families need guidance, education, and emotional support. What is more, government must not, through faulty policies, encourage desertion and the shirking of family responsibility.

It will not be easy to provide the necessary services. But if the rehabilitation of severely disadvantaged families requires them, then serious efforts must be made to provide them. It may well be, for example, that closer cooperation between public and private agencies is needed. It may also be that a greater expenditure of time and interest, as well as money, is required. If a mother in poor health is struggling to bring up three young sons, she needs money. But she also needs the help of some older man who will take a personal interest in her sons. For without such an interest they will have great difficulty growing up. This is where a private agency can be the most help. Much of what poor families need to rear their children can be bought with money. But much cannot.

Next to aiding the family, and probably because here the scope for social action is potentially much greater, the most important way to improve youth is to strengthen the school system. No matter how good its staff and curriculum may be, the school alone cannot insure that young people develop their potentialities to the optimum. Many young people, though they attend the finest schools, nevertheless fail to exert themselves and therefore fall short of expectations. Despite this important reservation, the fact remains that many young people are forced to attend, because of residence or limitations of parental income, schools that are conspicuously weak, whose staffs have limited academic competence and pedagogical skill. To compound matters, schools that are weak in staff are also likely to be weak in the depth of their curriculum. As a result, many pupils, in fact all but the exceptional, will fail to acquire the solid educational preparation necessary for college or a professional career. The crucial importance of the school for career development underscores the desirability of improving our nation's schools so that the brighter students will be stimulated to the point where they will be interested in pursuing their studies further and thus be enabled to take advantage of the opportunities open to them.

Although close to $20 billion is currently being spent on education, it is clearly inadequate to meet the minimum criteria set forth above. In many regions of the country the schools are grossly deficient—if assessed in terms of the proportion of pupils completing high school and continuing on to college. While some of these shortcomings may be due to community values which deprecate education, the nub of the difficulty more often is inadequate resources, both qualitative and quantitative. For the most part, the states and localities with the weakest schools are those with the lowest incomes and therefore with the lowest tax base. Even if the poorest states were to make—as many of them in fact do—a greater than average effort to raise additional school taxes, the yield from such efforts would not begin to approach what the richer states have available to spend on each child.

Historically, the support of public education has rested firmly on the states and localities. While such local control undoubtedly has substantial advantages, it should not be forgotten that for many generations children who have had the bad luck to be born into the poorer states and localities have been seriously discriminated against as a result. Several decades ago, most states, recognizing the different tax capacity of various localities, tried to equalize public support of education by assuring at least a basic minimum to each school district. But for various reasons, some good and many bad, this principle of equalization has not been extended to the national scene, although the prospects for substantial public aid to education are better now than at any time in the past. Considering the increased tendency of those born in the poorer states, especially in the South, to move into the more affluent sections of the country, the interest of the richer states in raising the educational levels of the low income states should be self-evident. For if the young people and the adults who migrate from the poorer to the richer states are inadequately educated, their value to the communities into which they migrate is substantially less than it might otherwise be. Help from the richer to the poorer states is called for not only on grounds of self-interest but also on grounds of equity and national survival. As we sought to make clear in *The Uneducated,* any sizable proportion of the draft-eligible population that is so poorly educated that it cannot answer the call to arms in a national emergency represents a danger that affects the entire population, rich and poor.

As far as equity is concerned, any increased expenditure on education by the poorer states will largely benefit the richer ones. The very affluence of the latter now attracts residents of the poorer states so that they have all of the expenses of education but few of the benefits. The richer states, for their part, should no longer acquire additions to their labor force without incurring some of the cost.

While improvement of the schools can contribute significantly to the more effective development of the young, it would be an error to assume that the school, even if it were well staffed, could meet the needs of all young people. For reasons outlined in an earlier chapter, a considerable proportion of young people, when they approach their fifteenth year, are no longer able, if they ever were, to profit from continuing exposure to books and classroom instruction. And the school workshop has not proved to be a satisfactory alternative for those who shy away from books.

What these youngsters badly need is an opportunity to work while learning. They will gain considerably from the exposure to adults, from the opportunity to earn money, and from being a part of a larger socially constructive undertaking in which they have a role, however minor. But, for the very reason that their formal schooling has terminated early they need subtle encouragement to continue studying, at least on a part time basis. They must be made to see, as they were unable to see while they were still in school, the connection between study, work, and the goals in life which they are interested in achieving.

But first and foremost they need a job—a paid job where they can acquire or deepen their limited skills. And this many, in fact most, are unable to find without a dreary, frustrating wait. Our society, long oblivious to the needs of this group, has placed barriers in their path, or else it has done little to enhance their chances of securing paid employment.

If the economy were operating at close to full employment, most sixteen-year-olds who wanted to work would have little difficulty finding a job. But the economy in recent years, even during periods of economic expansion, has been operating at somewhat less than full employment. Moreover, the immediate outlook for jobs is not promising. If anything, the disparity between jobs and job seekers in the absence of more vigorous government policies is likely to widen rather than to narrow. The federal government, however, is becoming increasingly aware of this surplus of job seekers, the result of the rise in the number of young people, the flow of women into the labor force, the dislocations brought about by an advancing technology, the continuing surplus of people on the farm, and still other factors. To the extent that the federal government adopts policies that will maintain a high level of employment, the job prospects of those who leave school early will be improved.

But special efforts are also needed. Employers and trade unions, for example, should review their admission, hiring, and training practices to see that they are not unnecessarily discriminating against young people who have not completed high school. And government, which is by far the largest employer in the country, should restudy its staffing policies to see what it can do to utilize at least some part of this young labor supply. The government should also explore the possibility of developing new training and intern programs. These programs could not only help solve the chronic manpower shortage in certain essential services, they could also enable young people to acquire the skills they sorely need in order to compete effectively in the labor market.

Other approaches also warrant study. Perhaps the Civilian Conservation Corps could be adapted to urban problems. We have never really considered, moreover, establishing training institutions for young people going into military service. Nor have we thought about how the armed services might contribute, over and above their primary defense mission to the training of the nation's manpower, especially the training of those young people for whom the conventional school has little to offer.

The challenge is clear. The solution may be difficult, but it is not beyond our imagination or our resources. The fact is that the school as it is presently constituted cannot meet the developmental needs of many adolescents. These young people need a chance to work, and to work for money. At a minimum they need an opportunity to enter a type of training program that fits their capabilities, which will provide them with at least a little cash, and which will help them to acquire the skills necessary for a better job later in life.

Another area in need of critical review is the policies governing compulsory military service. As noted earlier, the problem is one of equity. More young men are reaching military age than the armed services, active and reserve, require to fill their manpower needs. As a consequence, Selective Service regulations now grant deferments to those young men who are pursuing advanced studies, who are fathers, or who are engaged in work essential to the national interest. The first two grounds enable many young men to reach their twenty-sixth birthday without being called to active duty. Although technically eligible for service until they are thirty-five, they are seldom called once they have passed their twenty-fifth year.

The present system encourages many young men to gamble that they will not be called. Others try to balance out the relative advantages of enlisting for three or four years of active duty, allowing themselves to be drafted for two years, or joining a reserve or National Guard unit with the requirement that they serve for six months on active duty and five and a half years in the reserve. There are additional options, many of which are available only from time to time and most of which are available only to young men who have attended or have graduated from college.

While it simply is not practical to insist that all young men be treated the same with respect to military service, the inequities of the current system are greater than a democracy can tolerate. It will not be easy to devise, even after long and hard deliberation, a system which is fair and which will, at the same time, provide the armed services with the numbers and quality of manpower they require in a manner not too costly. But the need for reform is urgent, especially since, with an ever larger number of young men reaching military age, the inequities will become even greater in the future.

This nation has several choices. It can introduce a lottery to determine who among the eighteen-year-olds will serve and who will not. It can require nonmilitary service by those not needed in the armed services. It can reconsider the often rejected plan that every young man be given compulsory military training for four to six months, with a lottery choosing those to serve longer in order to meet the nation's minimum defense needs. Or it can weigh the various proposals that would alter the present balance between career and drafted personnel. Any of these suggestions, and they by no means exhaust the possibilities, would introduce greater equity into the present military manpower procurement system at little or no extra cost to our society. The subtle corruption involved in the present system is harmful to those who serve, to those who do not serve, and to the nation at large. Sharing the responsibility for the defense of the nation is basic to the integrity of a democracy. It would indeed be shortsighted to undermine it for reasons of expediency or economy.

The proliferation of educational institutions and curricula, the multiple options confronting young men with respect to military service, the large-scale return of married women to the labor market after their children grow up, and the even more rapid changes in nature of work; all these trends underline the importance of providing young people with adequate guidance services. Since their parents cannot hope to meet this need by themselves alone, the community must assume a large share of the responsibility.

There are those who believe that this responsibility can be met by the school. But teachers seldom possess the range of knowledge and experience necessary to cope effectively with the task of guidance, and even if more specialists were trained and placed in the educational system, it is still unlikely that the school could meet the responsibility in full. Teachers and guidance specialists can do a great deal—especially in the area of educational guidance. But much that needs doing does not logically fall within their competence or responsibility. Some of the most important guidance, as we tried to make clear earlier, is that proffered to parents before their children even enter school. In such cases, the pediatrician, the minister, or even the visiting nurse, may be much more influential. Later on, when school children reach the age of occupational discretion, they need to be exposed to individuals who are not only well-informed but also able to talk with young people and answer their questions about the opportunities available to them. Here the school counselor can play a strategic role. But well-informed and interested representatives of various occupational groups can also help.

If the foregoing analysis is correct, then the best way to increase the quality and the quantity of the guidance services available to preschool children, school children, and out-of-school young adults is to encourage the rapid expansion of the strong centers that already exist in the school, in certain private and voluntary organizations, and in various governmental agencies.

The various levels of government—federal, state, and local—can also make a contribution, either by providing essential materials, such as the *Occupational Handbook* prepared by the U. S. Department of Labor, or by providing testing and counseling services. The various profit, nonprofit, and voluntary agencies can also help. The needs are too great and the available resources too few to recommend that only one group be given jurisdiction.

While improved and expanded guidance services can be a great help, many young people need more than guidance. They are the children who are born with severe defects or who, though born normal, develop severe handicaps as a result of their early life experiences. Where the defects are serious and not likely to be outgrown in the course of time, society must face up to the challenge of providing these children with the extra services and help they need to compensate in whole or in part for their defects. Greater community action is needed to help the physically handicapped, the mentally retarded, the emotionally disturbed, and the aggressive child, just as soon as their deviations from the norm are recognized. For the earlier remedial action is begun, the more likely it is that the handicap will be eliminated or reduced and thereby prevented from crippling the child's chances for social growth and development. Regrettably, even major therapeutic and rehabilitative services will often be unable to eliminate serious pathology. But in many instances, an unfavorable trend can be corrected and frequently reversed.

While our society has made a considerable effort in recent

years to provide therapeutic and rehabilitative services for children in need of special help, there remains a wide gap between needs and resources. There also remains a wide gap between available resources and their effective utilization. What is needed is a rapid increase in the quality and quantity of these services: diagnostic and therapeutic child guidance clinics, programs for the mentally retarded child, efforts to enrich the life experiences of children from severely deprived homes, recreational opportunities for young people from urban slum areas, and similar programs aimed at arresting and, wherever possible, alleviating the impact of the serious personal and social handicaps which affect so many young people and which too often make a mockery of the claim that every child has a chance to develop his own potentialities to the fullest. While both additional funds and more trained personnel are required, something else is needed. Here, too, the volunteer has an important contribution to make. In fact, without his help it is unlikely that the requisite number of capable personnel can be obtained. In short, the improvement of youth requires more of a democratic society than the liberal expenditure of funds, important as such expenditure is.

This leads to the particular challenge facing the United States today: The widespread discrimination against minorities, particularly Negroes. For there can be no normal growth and development for Negro children in the face of widespread prejudice. To make matters worse, the white child growing up in a home or community rife with prejudice cannot escape unscathed. He too is harmed, though less seriously.

With Negroes accounting for more than ten percent of the population, and with other discriminated against ethnic and religious minorities accounting for a large percentage, prejudice strikes directly at a significant number of all the nation's children. No democracy seriously dedicated to improving the opportunities of young people can in good conscience continue to ignore, or take only small steps to rid itself of, the sin of racial, ethnic, and religious prejudice. This is not a matter of money, trained personnel, or any other resource in short supply. It is first and foremost a matter of conscience. It is not enough for a society to proclaim certain truths to be self-evident; it must act in accordance with those proclaimed truths. It is by their deeds, not by their words, that nations shall be judged.

By strengthening the family, the school, and guidance services, by eliminating the dross and deceit inherent in our present system of compulsory military service, by expanding the services available to the handicapped, and by exorcising the demon of prejudice—by all these ways and many more American society can reaffirm its conviction and commitment that free men can build a better world by providing more fully for their children.

It can do one more thing. It can take advantage of the potentialities of science. It can support and nurture science. In fact, the liberal support of science can eliminate old errors and uncover new truths, aiding in the complex task of charting a sound course for the improvement of youth. But the potentialities of science will be vouchsafed only to a people with a genuine love for truth and a willingness to live by it.

BIBLIOGRAPHY

All books have been published by Columbia University Press, except where other publishers are indicated.

Bray, Douglas W. *Issues in the Study of Talent.* 1954.
Committee on the Function of Nursing, Eli Ginzberg, chairman. *A Program for the Nursing Profession.* New York, The Macmillan Co., 1948.
Ginzberg, Eli. *Grass on the Slag Heaps: The Story of the Welsh Miners.* New York, Harper and Brothers, 1948.
—— *Human Resources: The Wealth of a Nation.* New York, Simon and Schuster, 1958.
—— *The Labor Leader.* New York, The Macmillan Co., 1948.
—— *A Pattern for Hospital Care.* 1949.
—— *Report on Manpower Utilization in Israel.* Jerusalem, Prime Minister's Office, 1961.
Ginzberg, Eli, and associates. *The Unemployed.* Harper and Brothers, 1943.
Ginzberg, Eli, et al. *The Ineffective Soldier: Lessons for Management and the Nation.* 1959.
Vol. 1: *The Lost Divisions.* With James K. Anderson, Sol W. Ginsburg, and John L. Herma.
Vol. 2: *Breakdown and Recovery.* With James K. Anderson, Sol W. Ginsburg, John L. Herma, and John B. Miner.
Vol. 3: *Patterns of Performance.* With James K. Anderson, Douglas W. Bray, Sol W. Ginsburg, John L. Herma, William A. Jordan, and Francis J. Ryan.
Ginzberg, Eli, assisted by James K. Anderson, Douglas W. Bray, and Robert W. Smuts. *The Negro Potential.* 1956.

Ginzberg Eli, Sidney Axelrad, Sol W. Ginsburg, and John L. Herma. *Occupational Choice: An Approach to a General Theory.* 1951.

—— and Hyman Berman. *The American Worker in the Twentieth Century.* New York, The Free Press of Glencoe, 1963 (in press).

—— and Douglas W. Bray. *The Uneducated.* 1953.

—— Sol W. Ginsburg, and John L. Herma. *Psychiatry and Military Manpower Policy: A Reappraisal of the Experience in World War II.* 1953.

—— and Ewing W. Reilley. *Effecting Change in Large Organizations.* 1957.

—— and Peter Rogatz. *Planning for Better Hospital Care.* 1961.

Ginzberg, Eli, ed. *The Nations Children.* 1960.

Vol. 1: *The Family and Social Change.*

Vol. 2: *Development and Education.*

Vol. 3: *Problems and Prospects.*

—— *Values and Ideals of American Youth.* 1961.

Ginzberg, Eli, chairman. *What Makes an Executive: Report of a Round Table on Executive Potential and Performance.* 1955.

Smuts, Robert W. *European Impressions of the American Worker.* 1953.

—— *Women and Work in America.* 1959.

National Manpower Council. Members of the Conservation of Human Resources Staff have contributed to the following publications:

A Policy for Scientific and Professional Manpower. 1953.

A Policy for Skilled Manpower. 1954.

Education and Manpower. ed., Henry David. 1960.

Government and Manpower. In press.

Improving the Work Skills of the Nation. 1955.

Proceedings of a Conference on the Utilization of Scientific and Professional Manpower. 1954.

Student Deferment and National Manpower Policy. 1952.

Womanpower. 1957.

Work in the Lives of Married Women. 1958.